# CURANDERISMO

## THE ART OF TRADITIONAL MEDICINE WITHOUT BORDERS

**SECOND EDITION**

ELISEO "CHEO" TORRES

**Kendall Hunt**
publishing company

Cover image courtesy of Dorene DiNaro
Interior images courtesy of the University of New Mexico unless otherwise noted.

**Kendall Hunt**
publishing company

www.kendallhunt.com
*Send all inquiries to:*
4050 Westmark Drive
Dubuque, IA 52004-1840

# CONTENTS

# AUTHOR'S BIOGRAPHY

Courtesy of Tim Sawyer.

Eliseo "Cheo" Torres began studying *curanderismo*, the art of traditional medicine, when he visited Espinazo, Nuevo Leon, Mexico, with his mentor, Dr. Stanley Bittinger, in the 1980s, and was fascinated with the Fidencista curandero festival. Soon after this experience, he met his teacher, Chenchito, and began studying the famous curandero Niño Fidencio. Since then, he has written several publications and books on the topic and has taught a number of courses on traditional medicine. His latest books on his life in traditional medicine and his research on the subject area are: *Curandero: A Life in Mexican Folk Healing* (2005) and *Healing with Herbs and Rituals: A Mexican Tradition* (2006). He also teaches a two-week course and an online class on the topic of *curanderismo*. His most recent courses are now offered online and this publication can be used to supplement these courses or be enjoyed by individuals who are not in the course.

# ACKNOWLEDGMENTS

As I wrote this book, I kept thinking and appreciating the commitment and generosity of the traditional healers from both Mexico and the United States. I was extremely blessed that my teacher and mentor of almost 30 years, Chenchito, was able to visit me in New Mexico at the age of almost 90 and share his knowledge and gentleness with the students at the University of New Mexico. You will enjoy reading about Chenchito and the Fidencista movement in Chapter 2, "*El Ultimo*: Chenchito, the Last of the Fidencista Healers."

The healers and their demonstrations highlighted in each chapter of this publication were video-taped by the talented staff from the University of New Mexico Extended Learning Information Technology Services. These employees have continuously supported me in offering online classes that concentrate on the topics presented in this book, and, because of that, this information can now serve as a supplement to these courses.

The staff in my office of Student Affairs have been helpful in supporting the *curanderismo* summer class with the majority of class logistics from registration to organizing the annual traditional health fairs. Dorene DiNaro has taken a number of excellent photographs of the healers throughout the years. Deyanira Nuñez supports the summer class as well as the online courses from beginning to end and ensures their success. Natalie Brigance helps with many of the logistics, and Cindy Mason with the finances—both of which are necessary to make the class run smoothly. I am also appreciative of the UNM Women's Resource Center for their co-sponsorship of the class and their dedication to ensuring the annual traditional health fair happens year after year.

In writing a publication, I always ask others to review it for their input in relating the correct message that I am attempting to deliver and for accuracies. I would like to thank four individuals who gave me their comments and they are Logan Sparks, Tonita Gonzales, Dorene DiNaro, and Nathan Lyons.

My final gratitude is for the many healers that have contributed to this book from Mexico, Africa, Peru, Puerto Rico, Cuba, and throughout the United States. I especially want to recognize two healers who help me plan the summer two-week class and also presented a number of topics in this publication. Rita Navarrete from Mexico City and Tonita Gonzales from Albuquerque, New Mexico, are multi-talented traditional healers and have positively impacted the lives of many people from students to community members. Their traditional health clinics support marginalized communities from Mexico and the United States and they have mentored a number of young professionals in the art and therapies of traditional medicine.

# INTRODUCTION

**M**y mother was not a *curandera,* a traditional healer, in the usual sense, but she knew much about medicinal herbs and healing rituals such as *mal de ojo*/evil eye, *susto*/fright, *empacho*/intestinal blockage, and other means of treating traditional illnesses. I often asked her to teach me and her answer was, "Learn as I do. I watched and practiced from my mother, just like she did with her mother. We didn't learn from books, but from word of mouth and practice." My mother was correct that these arts should be passed on orally, since there are not many publications on the art of traditional medicine. *Curanderismo* comes from the Spanish word *curar,* which means to heal. *Curanderos* are male healers, *curanderas* female, and the therapies of these traditional healers have survived hundreds of years. From here forward, we will vary the gender of the term, but keep in mind that a healer can always be of either gender, of course. Further, whenever the term "*curanderismo*" is used, we mean a traditional practice of healing mind, body, and spirit.

I have to admit that I was not a good student of my mother in learning about medicinal plants and rituals. These lessons became important to me once again when I met my mentor and teacher, Chenchito, 30 years ago, when he was at the age of 60. He has been a dedicated healer all of his life, and I continue following his teachings until his death in 2018 at the age of 90.

I introduced the topic of curanderismo at the University of New Mexico to students and the community 23 years ago, and have offered both two-week summer classes and online courses. I initiated these courses in collaboration with my friend and colleague, Dr. Arturo Ornelas, who, at the time, like me, was an administrator and professor. He was working at the University of Cuernavaca in Morelos, Mexico.

To my surprise, he was doing the same thing in Mexico with his students and community as I was in New Mexico. When planning the first curanderismo course, I decided, in partnership with the director of the University of New Mexico's Women's Resource Center, Sandrea Gonzales, to take a group of students during the summer to a holistic medicine school established by Dr. Ornelas. At that time, he was already leaving his job with a public university and devoting himself full-time developing his private traditional medicine school. After the first class in Mexico, and because of the cost of travel, I decided to offer a summer two-week class on the University of New Mexico Campus with Dr. Ornelas, where we would allow local healers from the area and out of state to help teach the first week of the course. The second week was to be taught by Dr. Ornelas and his designated curanderos(as), who were also professors at his school called *Centro de Desarrollo Humano Hacia la Comunidad*/Center for Human Community Development (CEDEHC). For more than 20 years, the summer class has been offered and has become popular within the university community, throughout the country, and outside of the United States. However, there are many students who cannot afford to travel and pay the expenses of the class. Therefore, in collaboration with the office of Extended Learning and their talented staff, I was able to develop an online course on curanderismo with the recordings of many of the healers who presented during the summer course. Two of the many healers who plan the courses with me during the year are Rita Navarrete from Mexico City, and Tonita Gonzales from Albuquerque, New Mexico. Students

**Figure I.1** Initiated by Dr. Arturo Ornelas and Dr. Eliseo "Cheo" Torres, the courses on Curanderismo of Mexico and the Southwest have partnered with lecturers from Mexico and the United States.

and those who are interested in curanderismo are encouraged to have an open mind and feel included with these teachings and practices that are offered through the two-week summer class, which offers some hands-on activities, or the online course, with demonstrations of a number of healing therapies and techniques.

In this book, you will be able to enjoy many of the traditional therapies that Rita and Tonita discuss and present as well as those demonstrated by a number of healers from throughout the United States and countries such as Uganda, Gabon, Peru, Cuba, and Puerto Rico. The staff in my university office, with the support of the Women's Resource Center, have contributed much to the success of these classes and this publication. They work behind the scene in registering students, organizing an herb walk at our local Botanical Garden, and assist in sponsoring a traditional health fair as part of the summer two-week curanderismo class.

Every culture on Earth has its own form of traditional healing, whether it references the herbs used for rituals and spiritual purifications in the Bible, the dietary guidelines set forth in Ayurvedic principles, or the drumming ceremonies of Native Americans. The study of curanderismo is a way of studying humanity, where one can recognize and connect with the entire global family. Although curanderismo draws on resources and aspects of healing traditions from Europe, Asia, and Africa, the primary sources described in the publication come from the Mexican indigenous traditions and from Spain, including its North African heritage. Since every culture has its own variation of healing, the primary goal of this book is to: (1) guide the reader toward an understanding of the concepts of curanderismo, (2) serve as a reference guide, indexing the healing modalities that define curanderismo, and (3) bridge the gaps between Western modern medicine and traditional healing. The author and a number of healers who contributed to this book stress that you, the reader, be aware of your comfort level and only pursue modalities that sound beneficial to you. Always consult with your primary care doctor first before taking any herb, tincture, or micro dosage, especially if you are already taking medication, in order to avoid drug interactions. What works for some people may not work for others, and there are numerous healing modalities to choose from. Everyone has their own comfort level with particular therapies, so if you are not comfortable getting an energetic/spiritual cleansing/*limpia,* fire cupping/*ventosa,* or doing certain ceremonies, or do not think it will benefit your sacred health, mind, or spiritual well-being, it is okay to not participate.

Throughout this book, we will explore several questions including: What is a limpia or energetic/spiritual cleansing? How do we compare a number of limpias from several different cultures such as Mayan, African, Cuban, and Puerto Rican? What are the concepts of diseases, ailments, and physical problems, and how do we treat, manage, and prevent them? What are the medicinal benefits offered by plants? Aside from the physical level, can we be healed on a spiritual and mental level?

It should be noted that the goal of this text is not to say that one healing modality is better than another or that traditional healing techniques are better than Western allopathic medicine. Herbs will not fix a broken leg in the way that Western medicine can, and Western medicine typically will not assess a person's physical, mental, and spiritual well-being in a three-dimensional approach the way most traditional healers will. Today we are seeing a shift in the way some doctors from Western medicine backgrounds treat patients, in that many are including traditional healing modalities and have incorporated those therapies into their practices.

This book is based on a number of videos recorded for the purpose of supporting the online classes on curanderismo. I have summarized the videos in each of the chapters, clarified some of the information, and added my own reflections and experiences to the themes. If the reader is enrolled in one of the online classes or the summer course, this publication will serve as a supplemental resource. This publication is useful to support a series of short Coursera classes as well as a number of workshops that I have offered in the past and hope to repeat in the future. I remind the reader that the themes on the topics are presented by experienced healers and, in my writings, I offer my opinions. Some of the material is historical or informational in nature and not meant to substitute for other allopathic treatments. The majority of the information comes from my experience in the field and the experts consulted here. Some other sources are added, as necessary.

This publication is divided into two parts. Part 1 emphasizes the traditional healing ways of Mexico and the Southwest. It begins with my mentor and teacher, Chenchito, and how he has impacted my life, especially in being humble and generous with others, but also how to appreciate the *Fidencista* traditional healing movement that has been around and thriving for more than 100 years. You will learn about the founder of the Fidencista movement and his unorthodox healing methods from one of the greatest curanderos called the "The Healer of Healers/*El Curandero de Curanderos*," Niño Fidencio, who died in 1938.

You will discover some popular medicinal herbs of the Southwest and learn from an internationally-known herbalist and friend, Dr. Tomas Enos, followed by two of my mentors, herbalists from Mexico (Doris and Lety) will be discussing herbs for the digestive and nervous systems. Tonita presents a chapter on using some of the plants mentioned by Tomas, Doris, and Lety. She prepares an alcohol-based tincture and a water-based *micro-dosis*, something akin to what we could call a "micro dosage," although there is no exact English equivalent. Rita and Tonita will show us the preparation of a number of fruits, nuts, and vegetable juices to prevent and to address certain ailments. Throughout the book, you will see the word limpia, which refers to a spiritual and/or an energetic body cleansing. Some may call it a soul or an aura cleansing, or alignment. Part 1 includes three types of cleansing by Laurencio, Velia, and Rita, which heal susto/fright. They will use different elements in performing their rituals such as an incense burner, *copal* resin incense, an egg, and plants. One of these elements used in limpias is also discussed in a chapter by Rita and Tonita on "Burning Incense for Harmonizing." You will experience a number of these spiritual cleansings throughout the book with the use of different elements by a number of healers from various cultures and countries.

Part 1 continues with a therapy for empacho, which means intestinal blockage and Tana, a healer and professor of traditional medicine from Mexico, will explain wet and dry empacho. *Manteadas* are a gentle healing massage using a shawl or a cotton cloth. This is a gentle therapy that has recently resurfaced after being popular years ago, and Rita will demonstrate how this technique is excellent for children, the elderly, and pregnant women. Rita and Tonita present an interesting chapter on "Healing with Fire, Earth, and Oils," addressing the ancient therapy of fire cupping/*ventosas*, which has now become popular with athletes in the Olympics to relax and alleviate muscle pain. Tonita demonstrates the usage of clay from the earth, in combination with lettuce, for skin problems, and Rita uses herbal essence oils in addressing delicate muscular spinal problems. Tonita and Rita also contribute a chapter on the Mexican *temazcal* sweat lodge, which has made a comeback, not only in Mexico, but also in the United States. We will see how the experience in a temazcal can address body, mind, and spiritual needs. Both are considered *temazcaleras(os)*, specialists in directing Mexican sweat lodges, and have incorporated them as part of their traditional health clinics. Part 1 ends with the chapter, "Healing with Laughter, Sound, and Music," with Rita demonstrating laugh therapy and the therapeutic benefits of laughter. Juan Carlos has perfected the use of sound vibrations using the sound of a conch shell combined with the power of the black shiny obsidian volcanic stone, while Elena will demonstrate a number of musical instruments and their unique vibrational sounds as used in a healing process including music therapy limpia.

Part 2 will emphasize the global perspectives and influences in curanderismo, beginning with a chapter on "The Influences of African Folk Healing," with the discussions by a group of traditional healers from Uganda, Africa, who spent a few days sharing their knowledge with the students in my summer class. During the same time, a second traditional African healer also joined us from the small country of Gabon. Bokaye will demonstrate the unique *mogongo* one-string instrument, and the *ngombi* harp used as part of his cultural spiritual and healing rituals. The next chapter discusses "The Influences of Afro-Latino Traditional Healing," beginning with a spiritual cleansing using dance and music and honoring the elements of fire, water, air, and earth. In the second subchapter, two *babalawos/santeros*/healers from Cuba demonstrate a traditional Afro-Latino limpia using a magical circle, herbs, coconut, and cigar smoke, with the final subchapter featuring a Puerto Rican Afro-Caribbean *Osain* spiritual cleansing by Dr. Ysamur Flores, a professor and a third generation practicing traditional medicinal and spiritual healer. In his spiritual cleansing, he uses a red and black fabric, plants and chants that have been part of the *Osain* healing tradition for hundreds of years. Mino, a healer and ambassador for the indigenous *Asheninka* community of the central jungles of Peru and his partner, Bernadette, an herbal instructor and director of Shabeta's Healing Garden in Albuquerque, present a chapter on "The Sacred Tobacco of Peru and Medicinal Plants for Women." Dr. Monica Lucero, a Doctor of Oriental Medicine demonstrates "The Use of Herbal Smoke for Healing" using the smoke and heat of the dried Mugwort plant prepared as a *moxa* stick, and a *moxa* box to alleviate muscular pains and open the meridian channels in the body. Most of us have sacred spaces whether they are in a church, chapel, in the woods, or on the beach. Rita and Tonita will share with us how they create their sacred space as part of their healing practices, which may be a space before entering a temazcal sweat lodge, or as part of a ceremony. The feather used by Native American traditional healing is an element that plays an important role with anthropologist Bob Vetter from New York. His spiritual and healing experiences among the Southern Plains tribes are part of his presentation in "Native American Feather Healing," where he shows us the power of feathers in native spiritual cleansings. The traditional bonesetter/*huesero* is practically extinct. However, Agustin Perez from Mexico City learned the trade of a bonesetter from his grandfather and father, and will offer a demonstration in the chapter, "Bonesetter (Huesero)."

Part 2 continues with the influences of the ancient Mayan culture and shows us how their acupuncture points are basically the same as those of Chinese therapies. Mexican traditional Acupuncturist Sofia will show us the traditional Mayan acupunctural points and how they used fish bones and maguey plant needles with garlic to sterilize them before puncturing the skin. Alex Jackson has studied the Mayan abdominal massage therapy with healers like Rosita Arvigo from Belize, Central America. He demonstrates this technique for problems related to the diaphragm, esophagus, liver, and colon. Two Mexican healers, Roberto and Felipa, perform similar body manipulative therapy as that of the bonesetter; however, their techniques are seen to be more similar to those of a chiropractor, as they demonstrate with body adjustments and alignments.

Rita is multi-talented with a number of healing modalities and she demonstrates a simple therapy of using water to heal in the chapter, "Hydrotherapy (Healing with Water)." We continue by discussing a number of limpias such as "*Tonalli* Cleansing," by Patricia Federico from Phoenix, Arizona. Rita returns to provide traditional healings concentrating on two stages of life whose health needs may not be completely met, which are for infants and the elderly, in a chapter titled, "Traditional Healing for Infants and the Aging Community."

The final chapter deals with a topic that is usually not discussed: death. The title of the chapter is, "Healing Grief through Day of the Dead (*Dia de Los Muertos*)." Dr. Anselmo Torres from Cuernavaca, gives us a brief history and meaning of one of the most popular celebrations in Mexico, Day of the Dead/ *Dia de los Muertos*, and the significance of the altar/*ofrenda* and how this tradition allows relatives and friends to celebrate, in a spiritual way, and help work out the stages of grief.

I hope that the chapter themes and information will give the reader a better understanding of traditional ways of healing the body, mind, and spirit and that it will offer an opportunity to compare the similarities and differences in traditional medicine from Mexico to that of African nations, Peru, Puerto Rico, Cuba, and China. I also offer some information on the roots of curanderismo, such as Native American culture, Middle Eastern and North African influences, and Mayan Mesoamerican traditions. I am pleased that many students as well as community members are interested in learning the medicine of their ancestors. Even medical schools are now incorporating traditional, complementary, or integrative medicine into their curriculum.

# PART 1

# CURANDERISMO IN THE SOUTHWEST AND MEXICO

# CHAPTER 1

# El Ultimo: Chenchito, the Last of the Fidencista Healers

I had met Cresencio Alvarado Nuñez, known as Chenchito, more than 30 years ago. I refer to him as "El Ultimo: Chenchito, the Last of the Fidencist Healers" before his death in 2018, he was possibly the only survivor who met the famous Niño Fidencio. There are hundreds of other Fidencista healers nowadays, who are practicing healers (curanderas/os) but were not alive during Fidencio's time. I met Chenchito through a university colleague of mine, Leo Carrillo. Leo was a close friend of his and suggested that I visit the village of Espinazo, Nuevo Leon, Mexico, where Chenchito owns a home and lives part of the year. Chenchito was also one of the organizers of a festival held in October and March in honor of the famous Mexican healer, Niño Fidencio. My family and I had been to one of the festivals before, and I wanted to return, especially knowing that I would meet and possibly stay a couple of days with Chenchito, a famous and true Fidencista (a follower of the healing movement) healer.

The first time I met Chenchito, he struck me as a handsome man, in his sixties, not even five feet tall, but with a huge smile, full of life, and very charismatic. I could feel Chenchito's unconditional love and innocence that reminded me of the descriptions of El Niño Fidencio, a simple man full of life, happiness, caring, and very charismatic. This description is of a characteristic that many of us have lost, especially in this new technical millennium that has us behind a desktop computer, an iPad, or an iPhone. My encounter with Chenchito was in the month of October, during the celebration of El Niño's death. Fidencio is often called El Niño, which is translated to "the child," but in this case is a term of endearment. The second celebration in Espinazo is in March, which is El Niño's saint's day.

Chenchito has two homes, one in the Mexican town of El Control, in the state of Tamaulipas, and the second one where El Niño lived, practiced his healings, and is buried: Espinazo, in the state of Nuevo Leon. It was in Espinazo, during the October Fidencista festival, that Chenchito invited me to spend two nights, sharing his humble one-room home with about 20 other guests. We all slept on the floor, and in spite of the large number of people sharing the room, I enjoyed a wonderful and restful night. I remember that during the night I got up at about 2 a.m. to go to the outhouse and saw Chenchito sitting at the kitchen table drinking a cup of hot herbal tea. The kitchen was outdoors, without walls and past a breezeway. When Chenchito saw me, he waved me over to join him. He said, "Cheo, let's visit since I can't sleep." He seemed full of energy at two in the morning and reminded me of the stories of El Niño who slept two or three hours a day because of his devotion to seeing as many patients as he could. Chenchito was anxious to share with me his stories, like the one that had recently happened to him. He said, "Cheo, a few weeks ago I was sick and thought I was dying. I laid in bed waiting for the final day and people came to visit me. I told them that I couldn't do any healings since my energy level was weak. I also started giving away my belongings. I gave away my food, my furnishings, and every material thing that I owned. When my home was completely empty, a lady came with her infant child who was very ill. She said, 'Chenchito can you help me with some money to see a doctor for my baby who is crying day and night? I don't know what's wrong with him.' I told the lady, 'I am sorry but I have nothing to give you since I've given everything away.' I thought for a minute and said, 'please bring me some pliers.' And she did, and I pulled my gold tooth and gave it to her saying, 'please take this and see how much you can get for it.' She left. Well Cheo, after two weeks, I decided I wasn't going to die, so I got back some of my food, the furniture, and most of my other belongings. Actually, I got back just about everything, except my gold tooth." After listening to this inspiring story, I realized that I was sitting next to a very caring, humble, and giving man with all of the characteristics of the folk saint, Niño Fidencio. When I say folk saint, I am not referring to a canonized, church-approved saint, but a saint created and designated by the people. Moreover, that is the title common folks have given to El Niño, and possibly to Chenchito in the near future.

During the time that I knew Chenchito, I worked at a university in South Texas, and I invited him to the campus to speak to the students in a class I was teaching. He made an impression on the students as he shared stories of the famous Niño Fidencio and even performed some spiritual blessings. Later on, I invited him to spend the night at my sister's home, and he agreed to do a number of healings in her lovely and lush outdoor garden. The word spread throughout her neighborhood that a famous curandero was visiting and doing healings. That evening, Chenchito must have had at least 50 people wanting to visit him and ask for advice on their illness. Chenchito blessed everyone that evening and performed spiritual/energetic cleansings using eggs, lemons, and plants to sweep the body of negative vibrations while praying and chanting. The belief behind the spiritual/energetic cleansing is that the egg and lemon absorb negative vibrations from the body, while aromatic plants such as Rue, Basil, and Rosemary sweep away the unwanted vibrations. During his healings, he would prescribe certain plants for whatever was ailing the person, and I, as his assistant, would take notes on a piece of paper and hand it over to the person after the treatment. I was walking next to Chenchito who had channeled the spirit of El Niño Fidencio and was performing the healings while in a trance. It was as if El Niño was present.

After that time, 20 years ago, I left South Texas and began my new employment at the University of New Mexico in Albuquerque, as an administrator and professor. About five years after beginning my new job, I taught the first class in New Mexico on curanderismo. During this time, I phoned a friend in Texas and asked about Chenchito and was told that he had passed away. I was sad and remembered a loyal friend and great mentor. I thought for a minute that if he had been alive now, he would be about 90 years old. So naturally, because of the age, his death made sense to me.

And yet, later, I received a phone call from a woman named Margarita who lives in Roswell, New Mexico. Margarita said, "Cheo, you don't know me but we both have someone in common. We know Chenchito, a curandero from Mexico. My mom has been very sick and she asked that we bring Chenchito from Espinazo, Mexico, to see her in Roswell and he is right here, next to me and wants to talk to you." I almost fainted, thinking that Chenchito was dead. And so what a surprise it was to hear his voice say, "Cheo, I heard you are now living in Albuquerque, New Mexico, and I have been dreaming about you and want to see you." My quick response was, "Of course, my dear Chenchito. Please come see me." But I thought for a moment and said, "Why don't you wait until July and come see me during the class I teach on curanderismo?, and you can meet my students." Chenchito's reply was, "Yes, I'll be there." I thought, "Chenchito is 90 years old and probably won't come to Albuquerque since he doesn't fly, and he will travel by car and will take about 20 hours to get here." However, I was wrong. Two weeks before the beginning of my class in July, Margarita called me and said, "I am ready to go to Espinazo to pick up Chenchito, and we will be at your home on Saturday." When he and Margarita arrive at my home, I could not believe that Chenchito was 90 years old. He looked that same as when I first met him 30 years ago. The differences that I noticed were more gray hair and a slower walk, but he still was full of energy and ready to heal and touch the lives of our students and the community.

After a restful night, Chenchito was ready to visit the classroom of about 200 excited students. I had prepared the students for Chenchito's visit telling them about the Fidencista movement, how El Niño Fidencio had selected Chenchito's mother as one of his disciples in the early 1920s, and how Chenchito had lived the teachings and doctrines of the Fidencista movement all of his life. When Chenchito entered the classroom, all

200 students were silent, and you could hear a pin drop. I called for a 15 minute class break and many students ran to Chenchito during this time and some began crying as they held his hand. I believe that the students felt a powerful and loving energy that is hard to explain unless you meet those unique individuals that have a certain gift; it is called a *don* in Spanish and Chenchito has it. Soledad Woodburn is known as Chole and one of Chenchito's helpers. She describes him as a holy person possibly with the characteristics of Mother Teresa or Gandhi.

Chenchito spent a week with the students, many community members, and with my family. He was accompanied by two loyal assistants, Margarita, who brought him from Mexico, and Chole who traveled from Indiana to be with him. Chole shared a story of when she met Chenchito. Her mother was very sick and appeared to be suffering from an infection on her leg. She arrived at Chenchito's home in the late evening and was quickly assisted by

**Figure 1.1** Chenchito performing blessing on student, Sandra Torres.

Chenchito. He gathered a large amount of the *Gobernadora* plant, also known as *Hediondilla,* which translates to "smelly" because of its strong odor. In English, we know it as **Creosote Bush** or **Chaparral**. It is considered an excellent plant for infections, and it thrives well in the desert arid area of Chenchito's hometown of Espinazo. The *Gobernadora* was boiled for a few minutes. Chenchito soaked a cloth in the hot strong fragrant liquid and placed the hot cloth compress on the lady's infected leg all night. By morning, Chole's mom was feeling much better and continued the treatment for several more days. Instead of losing her leg to amputation, she was completely healed and she lived a healthy life for more than 20 years. In gratitude for the healing, Chole and her mom returned to Espinazo once or twice a year to visit Chenchito, often submerging the lady's body in el *Charquito*, or the miraculous pond, which will be described later on in this chapter.

In addition to describing the story of her mother's healing, Chole also shared with me how she had humbled herself when visiting Chenchito and had slept next to him with others on the floor at his humble home in Espinazo. I understood what Chole was saying since I have experienced the same scenarios, Chole also mentioned that Chenchito keeps the names of all that he has met, including the names of my students, and that he prays for all before going to sleep. Chenchito claims that, as a child, he met the Niño Fidencio in the year 1945, but I suspect that he actually met a healer channeling the spirit of the famous healer since Fidencio died in 1938. Since Fidencio's death, hundreds of healers, including Chenchito, continue the healings and practices as if they were El Niño Fidencio, channeling the spirit of the famous healer. All of the healers consider themselves *materias* (or mediums) that channel the spirit of El Niño Fidencio, or they call themselves, *cajitas* (small boxes). I asked Chenchito why he and other healers call themselves cajitas and his answer was, "We call ourselves cajitas because our body is a box that holds our soul in order to receive the spirit of El Niño Fidencio."

Throughout the years that I have known Chenchito, he has shared with me the rich life and contributions of Niño Fidencio, beginning with the story of how his mother was one of Fidencio's disciples and student. He talked about his two dear friends, colleagues, and healers, Fabiola and Panita. They were, like Chenchito, children during the time of Fidencio's popularity in the town of Espinazo.

As I have researched El Niño Fidencio's life, I have learned that he was born in 1898 and given the name of José Fidencio de Jesus Sintora Constantino and died on October 19, 1938. During his lifetime, he touched and healed thousands of lives in the small dusty village of Espinazo, Nuevo Leon, Mexico. A documentary film by Nicolas Echevarria named *Niño Fidencio: The Miracle Healer of Espinazo* produced in 1980 and an interview with his brother, Joaquin Constanino Sintora, offer the highlights of Fidencio's accomplishment between the years 1921 until his death in 1938. (Echevarria, 1980) Fidencio has been described as a miracle healer because of his miraculous and incredible healings, and a person with telepathic and clairvoyant abilities because of his intuitive and perceptive capacity to see people, thoughts, and experiences beyond our senses. He also used unorthodox methods of healing such as surgeries with pieces of broken glass rather than a scalpel knife. During his healings, he hired musicians and danced and laughed with his patients, believing that laughter was part of the healing process. Similarly, we now have an innovative treatment called, "Laugh Therapy." To punish those that had broken the law with acts such as abuse of family, rape, and robbery, he would throw them in a cage with a live leopard. The person was so scared that he or she promised to change and never repeat the offense, not knowing that the animal was toothless and clawless. In addition, some of his treatments were the use of a common swing, water therapy, and medicinal plants. He practiced midwifery, delivering a large number of babies. It is said that, at times, all 30 cots used as beds were occupied in his maternity ward.

Most of his followers arrived to the town of Espinazo by train, just like the President of Mexico, General Plutarco Elias Calles, did in 1928. Fidencio received the President at the train station and met with him for about six hours. No one knows if the President or his daughter was ill. What was known is that the press was there and publicized the event in the newspapers and added to Fidencio's popularity. During this time, the small village of Espinazo grew into a tent city with a population estimated at 40–50 thousand inhabitants living in temporary tents.

The ritual when arriving to Espinazo, which continues as a custom until today, is to circle the ***Pirulito*** tree with song and prayer. The Pirulito is a Pirul tree (also called ***Piru)*** where El Niño Fidencio would meet and welcome, under its green shade, the multitude of followers who came for a healing or just a blessing. The belief is that the original Pirul tree was brought from the country of Peru, by the Spaniards, to Mexico and California, where it is referred to as the **California Pepper Tree,** *Schinus molle*. The fruit, sap, and bark of the tree are used for treating wounds, urinary infections, and tooth and gum problems. It is also used to sweep the body in a spiritual or energetic cleansing. The original tree, treasured by Fidencio and his followers, died and was replaced by a second ***Pirulito*** that now has its own caretaker and continues greeting the many visitors to Espinazo including groups of organized Fidencistas called ***misiones***, many times with their own established temples or churches found throughout Mexico and parts of the United States. The missions are led by a healer, not referred to as a curandero(a), but rather called materia, (medium) or cajita (small box) as I explained earlier in this chapter via Chenchito's definition of a cajita.

After greeting the ***Pirulito***, the misiones process in, many with their musicians and led by a materia or cajita dressed like a holy person with a white tunic and a red or turquoise colored bandana, with a matching colored hat. Other believers crawl, roll, or walk on their knees down a dirt dusty street called **Penance Road** or *Camino de Penitencia*. They are all on their way to El Niño Fidencio's burial tomb. At the tomb, which is in a chapel, they are greeted by some caretakers that receive flowers, candles, and religious offerings and place them on an altar. One can also view a number of photographs of Fidencio, including one of his body in a coffin that resembles how he looked at the time of his death on October 19, 1938.

After the followers visit the tomb with a personal tribute, prayer or song to Fidencio, some choose to walk to a muddy trough called *El Charquito*, which means "the puddle." Here you see a

**Figure 1.2** The multitude of Nino Fidencio's followers arrive to the town of Espinazo, Nuevo Leon are welcomed by the Pirulito Tree.

diversity of materias of all ages and genders dressed in the traditional white tunics with different colored kerchiefs and hats indicating their allegiance to a particular *mision* or **mission group**. The materias submerge the sick patients in the muddy and miraculous water while chanting and praying. This is the same pond where Fidencio is said to have bathed lepers. In addition to the *Charquito* experience, Fidencio would also use water as a therapy (which we now call **Hydrotherapy**) for treating pain and blood circulation by using different water temperatures. Water therapy is still used by some of the healers that I know, and I enjoy a similar therapy at Ojo Caliente Mineral Springs. This is a healing place that opened in 1868 and is located northern New Mexico, where I soak in natural hot pools containing the healing minerals of Lithia,

**Figure 1.3** In the early 1900s, El Nino Fidencio would jump on the large crowd of followers. His popularity could be compared to that of a rock concert.

Iron, Soda, and Arsenic. During my soaking, I remember what it must have been like during Fidencio's water treatment therapies of yesteryear.

As you walk the streets of Espinazo, you see a number of materias surrounded by people seeking a blessing or a particular healing or advice. Some of the materias are tossing fruit and candy at the crowed, the same as Fidencio did during the years 1927–1929, in the pinnacle of his popularity. It was believed that if you caught the apples or oranges tossed by Fidencio and ate them, you would be blessed and it would help in the healing process. During these years, the multitudes were so large that they resembled a popular rock concert where Fidencio would jump on the crowd and they would roll his body overhead throughout the multitude of people.

As you continue exploring Espinazo, you see people of all ages enjoying a swing called *El Columpio*, a replica of the one Fidencio used for treating certain illnesses, including the illnesses of people suffering from extreme stress. There is even the story of a mute who was asked to stand in front of the swing. Fidencio rocked in the swing and bumped the man several times so that the person became so angry that he found the voice he had lost in order to curse the healer.

On one of my trips to visit Chenchito, I joined other pilgrims during the Fidencista festival on a pilgrimage from the village of Espinazo to a nearby mountain, called *Cerro de la Campana* or **Bell's Mountain**. Many of the pilgrims are led by a materia, and it was at this mountain that El Niño Fidencio would meditate and pray on his knees. Believers compare this event to that of Jesus Christ in the Garden of Gethsemane, where he prayed before his crucifixion. Now pilgrims make the journey on foot to the mountain in a way resembling other pilgrimages held throughout Mexico and parts of the United States, and other countries during Good Friday, a day of fasting and penance, just before Easter Sunday. I continue a similar pilgrimage every Good Friday for a 12-mile walk to the **Santuario de Chimayo** in northern New Mexico, which was founded in the early 1800s. My objective is to arrive to the shrine, to pray, and to gather holy dirt located in a small room adjacent to the altar. There is a small round pit in the center of this room where I take the miraculous dirt and place it in a plastic bag and use it during the year for a number of illnesses. The Chimayo annual ritual reminds me of my pilgrimage to **Bell's Mountain** and the holy water in *El Charquito* of Espinazo, Mexico.

As I ponder the unorthodox treatments of Chenchito and Niño Fidencio, I realize that both healers were brilliant and, possibly, ahead of their time. These two healers were simple folk, yet very charismatic, and creative in their healings. They touched the lives of thousands of believers from both Mexico and the United

**Figure 1.4** Chenchito, at the age of almost 90, continues his mission of healing, similar to that of El Niño Fidencio.

States. They devoted their life to serving others and never made a profit for their services. Whatever was given to them, they gave to the poor and needy. I know this because I have seen Chenchito give anything he has to those in need and he continues to live the life of poverty. He is a Gandhi or Mother Teresa, as Chole says above. In my opinion, both Chenchito and Fidencio are the curanderos of curanderos that have touched the lives of thousands. It is difficult to believe that the Fidencista movement has continued to survive nowadays, 80 years after the death of El Niño Fidencio. As Chenchito told me, "The Fidencista movement has become a selfless religion of common folks that continue helping others and expecting nothing in return."

# CHAPTER 2
# Introduction to Medicinal Plants

Plants, especially those for medicinal use, have always been part of my culture. Since the beginning of mankind, plants have been used for ornamentation, food, and medicine. I suspect that man and woman learned the usage of medicinal plants by observing animals, which seem to have an instinct for consuming plants for their illnesses, or they may have learned through trial and error, experimenting with the herbs. My interest in herbology is focused on the usage of the medicinal plants of Mexico and the Southwest. It is difficult to identify some of these plants because of the many variations in common names, in English as well as Spanish, according to region, but they all have only one universal botanical scientific name. In Mexico, the usage of these plants has remained part of the culture, with *botanicas* or *yerberias*/herb stores found in just about every village and city. One of the most impressive yerberias is located in the famous *Mercado Sonora*, a traditional market located near the historical district of Mexico City. I have gone to this market place with my friend and healer from Mexico City, Rita Navarrete, early in the morning, and have been amazed with the many fresh medicinal plant stalls throughout the market, where you can find just about any plant you want. With the large number of Mexican immigrants now living in the United States, there is a resurgence of Mexican herb stores (especially in the Southwest) and every large city, such as Houston, San Antonio, Dallas, Los Angeles, Chicago, Denver, Phoenix, Albuquerque, and New York. Because of the diversity of these large communities, Latinos are using the varieties of herbs found in these cosmopolitan cities, not only those from Mexico or Latin American countries, but also plants from India and China. In Part 2 of this book, we will discuss the influences that have become part of curanderismo including medicinal plants and rituals used by healers from Africa and various Latin American countries such as Peru, Cuba, and Puerto Rico, as well as Mexico.

My mother treasured her medicinal plants and treated them as part of the family. I grew up knowing to respect and nurture these plants that could someday save our lives. My mother's medicinal garden was spread throughout her yard, among the flowers and vegetables, many times in old coffee cans used as pots. When neighbors and relatives would visit, the first conversation was about medicinal plants along with an herbal walk, talking about and pointing to the different plants and their healing properties. Before the guests left our home, they were given cuttings of some of the plants and those with their roots were transplanted to old tin cans or just placed in burlap sacks.

Throughout the years, I have expanded my knowledge of medicinal plants, learning from expert herbalists that contribute to this chapter such as my good friend, Dr. Tomas Enos from Santa Fe, New Mexico. He devotes his life to studying herbology and teaching others the science and knowledge of plants, especially those of the Southwest. I have learned from three wonderful mentors and teachers from the Mexico City area. First Doris Ortiz, who is a walking Wikipedia on medicinal plants, knowing the common and botanical names of hundreds of medicinal plants. In subchapter 2.2, she will discuss a number of plants for the digestive system. It is a system that turns our food, throughout the day, into nutrients that our body needs for survival. Doris knows a variety of plants that can heal the main organs in the digestive system, which includes the stomach, large and small intestines, liver, gallbladder, and pancreas.

My second mentor, who will discuss plants for the nervous system, is Leticia (known as Lety) Amaro Velázquez, a holistic healer for almost 20 years. The nervous system, which includes the brain and spinal cord, is our complex human computer, something that Lety understands. She prescribes plants to help repair some of damaged symptoms of anxiety disorders, stress, and depression, as well as facial pain, and so on.

My third teacher is Rita Navarrete, whom I have known for about 16 years. She is part of the curanderismo class that I teach as a two-week summer course. This is in addition to two, three-month-long online classes and four, six-weeks in duration, Massive Open Online Classes (MOOC) on Coursera. A second colleague, who partners with Rita on these classes, is my friend and colleague, Tonita Gonzales. She is originally from Gonzales Ranch in northern New Mexico but now has a successful holistic medicine clinic and a Mexican Sweat lodge (Temazcal) in the North Valley of Albuquerque, New Mexico. In this chapter, Rita and Tonita discuss the preparation of tinctures and microdosis. The tinctures are alcohol-based liquid extracts from plants while the microdosis are less concentrated water-based using a smaller percentage of the tincture.

These four subchapters: "Plants of the Southwest," "Medicinal Plants for the Digestive System," "Medicinal Plants for the Nervous System," and "Tinctures and Microdosis" will describe a variety of traditional usages of plants in order to treat a number of illness. The information on the usage of these curative plants is offered by five practitioner and holistic healers who have been studying and practicing traditional medicine in Mexico and the United States for many years. I have added my own knowledge of herbs, and comments, to the four subchapter articles as well as to the other chapters of this book.

The information on the medicinal herbs discussed in this chapter and other parts of this book is for information only and please be reminded to consult a professional herbalist or your physician if you are taking medication, in order to avoid complications and possible drug interactions.

## 2.1 PLANTS OF THE SOUTHWEST

I met Dr. Tomas Enos a few years ago when he was researching the plant that is commonly known by the name of *Chaya* or Spinach Tree, with the botanical name of *cnidoscolus chayamansa*. Dr. Tomas Enos from Santa Fe, New Mexico, has his PhD in ethnobotany and is president of Milagro Herbs Inc., where he works with a large number of organic and wild harvested plants. A few years ago, he did a two year apprenticeship in one of my favorite cities, Oaxaca, Mexico. His study was on traditional healing practices, as well as ethnobotanical research, in Mexico, and later in Central and South America. Dr. Enos has also established the Milagro School of Herbal Medicine, which offers both a resident and online program on herbalism and therapeutics. Dr. Enos lectures during my two week summer class and my online courses on curanderismo.

During his presentations in the online class, he discusses Native American contributions to the history of herbal medicines that date back thousands of years. He mentions how these traditions changed with the arrival of Spaniards and Africans to the Americas. Dr. Enos emphasizes that, before using these plants, one needs to talk with someone who is well schooled on how to use them and prepare them. The following medicinal plants of the Southwest are only a few of Dr. Enos' favorite ones, that he describes in his lectures to the students enrolled in my class, "Traditional Medicine Without Borders: Curanderismo in the Southwest and Mexico." The name of the following plants will start with the English common name(s), followed by their universal botanical scientific name, and the Spanish common name(s). Some of the plants may have more than one English and Spanish common name.

**Figure 2.1** Dr. Tomas Enos, herbalist, describes medicinal plants of the Southwest.

1. **Swamp Root**, *Anemopsis californica*, **Yerba Mansa/Bavisa/Swamp Root/Lizard's Tail**. One of Dr. Enos' favorite plants, **Yerba Mansa**, grows along small streams and rivers, since it likes swamps and wet places and is harvested in the fall. It has anti-inflammatory properties, is excellent for an upset stomach and any kind of inflammation of the throat, colon, or stomach. The traditions in the usage of the plant are cross cultural, similar in New Mexico and Mexico. **Yerba Mansa** is a creeper plant, with an aromatic and beautiful fragrant white flower.

2. **Pine Pitch/Resin**, *Pinus edulis*, **Trementina/Aguarras**. This is one of New Mexico's popular remedies specific to the state's native Piñon Pine tree. Dr. Enos gathers the **Trementina** pitch or resin, dries it, and grinds and adds it into the preparation of a number of topical recipes for skin rashes, cuts, and possible infections, since it acts as an antibiotic. I have used the resin added to an ointment to draw out a splinter in my hand that was bothering me for days. I rubbed the ointment where the splinter was at night, and by morning the splinter was pulled out. I have known of people using the **Trementina** resin for rheumatic painful joints and taking a small dose internally for dry and sore throat and for bronchitis. In Mexico, the pitch is also called *aguarras*.

3. **Silktassel**, *Garrya* spp., **Cuachicheek** (Native-American). This shrub grows prolifically in dry land and has resiny tough leaves. The plant is used as a tea or in an alcohol tincture for a variety of stomach, intestinal, and menstrual cramps, since it is a muscle relaxant and relieves pain. It is recommended that about 40 drops 2–3 times a day be used as a liquid extract tincture. In some developing countries, this powerful plant was used as a substitute for Quinine in treating malaria.

4. **Oshá or Bear Medicine or Indian Parsley**, *Ligusticum porteri*, **Chuchupate**. It belongs to the parsley family and is one of the most well known and loved medicinal plants in Northern New Mexico, growing in the mountains more than 8,000 feet above sea level. **Osha** is used in California and Colorado as well as in Mexico and has antibiotic, antimicrobial effects, and strengthens the immune system. Some carry this plant with them in their pant pocket in the fall season and chew it to prevent colds and the flu. Others use it for the respiratory systems, especially for clearing the lungs and allergies. Dr. Enos prepares liquid extracts of this **Oshá** or steeps it in honey for oral consumption. He also prepares an ointment with **Oshá** to warm certain parts of the body. Cowboys and Native Americans have used this plant for many years and some place the root of this plant in their medicine bag for good luck and to ward off evil and they will keep pieces of it in their boots to ward off rattlesnakes. Many homes, especially where the plant grows, keep it in their medicine kits. Since this plant is difficult to cultivate and is picked in the wild in the high mountainous areas, one should be careful and not confuse **Oshá** with the poisonous hemlock because of their resemblance.

5. **Aloe vera**, *Aloe barbadensis*, **Sabila**. Some refer to the **Aloe vera** as the miraculous plant or *la plantita milagros*, and my mom would say, "It cures everything from pimples to wrinkles." Indeed, she would use it on her face for wrinkles and on ours for pimples. The gel, after peeling the green long leaf, is where the healing properties are and it is often used for burns and sunburns and I always keep several potted plants and place them in my outdoor porch in the summer and indoors in the winter. It is believed that this plant protects your home and that it absorbs negative vibrations from certain guests visiting your home. I have also added the fresh gel to fresh papaya fruit, blended it with a few ice cubes and water and consumed it for digestive problems, including diverticulitis, and it has been very beneficial. Some take the Aloe vera juice to eliminate toxins and cleanse the body of impurities. Aloe vera is used as an excellent cooling treatment for hot conditions, since many believe in the hot and cold theory of illnesses. This is based in an ancient Greek belief in humors, from which come certain practices. You use cold plants to treat hot illnesses and hot plants to treat cold ailments, for example.

6. **Sagebrush/Desert,** *Artemisia tridentata,* **Salvia/Chamiso Hediondo. Salvia** is soothing and aromatic and used for stomach ailments and parasites. It is an antiseptic plant that fights infections. Some add it to their bath water and believe that it helps with their arthritis and alleviates pain.

7. **Creosote Bush/Chaparral,** *Larrea tridentata,* **Gobernadora/Hediondilla.** The Spanish term *Hediondilla* means smelly or stinky because of its very aromatic strong smell. It is bitter and helps those with liver, gall bladder conditions, and kidney disorders. In fact, many bitter medicinal plants are used for these conditions. This plant is also used for pain, arthritis, and the digestive tract. Because of its strong properties, Dr. Enos recommends that one should prepare **Creosote Bush** as a weak tea, only steeping it for a few minutes, and drink it 2–3 times a day. This desert plant grows well in the Southwest part of the United States and arid areas of Mexico and is considered a diuretic, expectorant, antiseptic, antioxidant, antiviral, and antibiotic.

8. **Chili pepper,** *Capsicum* sp.,***Chilipitin.*** Hot peppers have been used since pre-Hispanic times not only as an excellent condiment, but also as medicine. The native pea-sized hot pepper is called *Chilipitin* and is ferociously hot. They can be ground and sprinkled on food, added to a tomato paste, or just steeped in oil or vinegar and used on meats and vegetables. This pepper grows well in the dry and arid regions of Southern Arizona, Texas, and Northern Mexico and is consumed more in the fall and winter to help keep warm and to stimulate the circulatory system, the heart, and strengthen a sluggish digestive system. It is an anti-inflammatory and believed to release capsaicin and endorphins, the body's natural painkillers, and is used topically for pain and joint issues.

Three medieval medicinal plants with Mediterranean roots brought to the Americas by the Spaniards are: Rosemary, Oregano, and Lavender. The European influence of medicinal plants has been a part of southwestern herbalism since the conquest expanded in this region. When the Spaniards arrived in the Americas they brought with them plants that were native to Spain or had been brought to that country by the Moors, who had been in Spain some 800 to 1,000 years (Trotter and Chavira, 2011). Much of this knowledge of plants was merged with indigenous knowledge by both the Spanish and the native peoples. We see part of this process in, for example, the Codex Badiano (Gates, 2012). Many of these plants needed small amounts of water and lots of sunshine, such as the following three plants. They also have great aromas and are not only excellent condiments for everyday cooking but also can be used for medicine as described below:

1. **Rosemary,** *Rosmarinus officinalis,* **Romero.** This plant thrives in New Mexico, Texas, California, and Arizona, and is utilized for a number of illnesses. **Rosemary** leaves in a tea are used to improve memory and are an antioxidant, disinfectant, antibacterial, prevents infections, and they are used for skin, hair, and scalp conditions. They are also used for delayed menstruation and some digestive disorders.

2. **Wild Marjoram,** *Origanum vulgare,* **Oregano.** Not only is **Oregano** an excellent food condiment for many Italian and Mexican dishes, but it is also used (especially **Oregano Oil)** for respiratory ailments, sore throat, coughs, and the symptoms associated with a cold, since it has antibacterial and anti-inflammatory qualities. Some use it for indigestion and seasickness.

3. **Lavender,** *Lavandula* sp., **Lavanda/Alhucema.** The Spanish name **Alhucema** is derived from the Arabic language and there are a number of varieties that are cultivated, especially in arid regions. The pleasant aroma of **Lavender** is antidepressant, and the flowers are good for infections, a mouth rinse, gum problems, and even menstrual cramps, since it is an antiseptic and sedative with the ability to numb pain. It is excellent for digestion, intestinal gas, and is considered antiemetic, which indicates it will stop vomiting. It is used in a number of cosmetics such as lotions, creams, and oils.

## 2.2 MEDICINAL PLANTS FOR THE DIGESTIVE SYSTEM

Adoración Ortiz, known as Doris, is one of the most knowledgeable herbalists I have ever met. I was fortunate to take a class with her on herbology a few years ago. I was impressed to learn that my teacher, Doris, not only knew the common name and usage of the medicinal plants, but she also memorized hundreds of their scientific botanical names. She believes that the body's nervous system affects the digestive system and that stress is the greatest cause of most illnesses. She also believes that certain emotions are the culprits of a number of ailments, such as the lack of love being related to diabetes: a person no longer sees the sweetness of life and substitutes it for an excess of sweetness in foods, which impacts our kidneys. She discuss how chronic constipation is caused by being inflexible, wanting to be too much in control, and not being able to let go of certain things. The plants described

**Figure 2.2** Herbalist, Doris, discusses the medicinal plants for the digestive system.

in this chapter are only a few that Doris gathered from the University of New Mexico's lush gardens. The native trees and plants throughout the beautiful campus are considered an arboretum, with labels indicating the names of the trees and plants. Doris decided to select a few of these plants from the university gardens that she uses for the digestive system such as:

1. **Periwinkle**, *Vinca minor,* **Vinca**. She states that in Mexico, Vinca is used to treat certain cancers, possibly because this plant improves the immune system, promotes healing, and purifies the blood. Vinca alkaloids are actually used today in chemotherapy. She finds that these herbs also help with the digestive system, which also impacts diabetes.

2. **Basil,** *Ocimum basilicum,* **Albahaca**; **Brook Mint,** *Mentha arvensis,* **Poleo**; **Mugwort,** *Artemisia vulgaris,* **Estafiate**; and **Spearmint,** *Mentha spicata,* **Yerbabuena** are all used for gastritis, which is caused by inflammation of the lining of the stomach, with the symptoms of nausea, burning sensations, and stomach pain. Doris' remedy for gastritis is to drink three cups of cold spearmint tea daily.

3. **Basil, Brook Mint, Mugwort,** and **Rosemary** are also taken as a blood protector and remove fats from the liver in addition to lowering the cholesterol levels.

4. **Lily,** *Lilium* sp. Azucena/Lirio is a plant found in many home gardens and can be used medicinally for relaxing the nervous system, which impacts the digestive system.

5. **Dandelion,** *Taraxacum officinale,* **Diente de León** eliminates fats and stimulates the liver and kidneys, since it has diuretic and anti-inflammatory qualities.

6. **Marigold/Aztec Marigold/Mexican Marigold,** *Tagetes erecta,* **Cempasúchil.** This **Marigold** is used to control diabetes, an illness that has killed more people than world wars, according to Doris, and she recommends a cup of the petals boiled with a lime cut in quarters at 11:00 p.m. to help in controlling the glucose level in the blood. This plant has anti-inflammatory and antiseptic qualities and is the same flower that is used during celebrations of the Day of the Dead, where it is taken to the cemeteries and altars.

7. **Cactus/Prickly Pear,** *Opuntia* sp., **Nopal** is blended as a smoothie drink with a **Tomatillo,** *Physalis philadephica,* known as a Mexican husk green tomato, and is taken before a meal in order to lower the

glucose levels of the body. While working at Texas A&M University-Kingsville in South Texas, a university colleague of mine was researching the usage of young tender cactus pads called **Nopalitos** in controlling type 2 diabetes. According to Doris, another remedy to lower blood sugar levels is to blend seven green beans with water and drinking it before or with your meals.

8. **Walnut Tree**, *Juglans* sp., **Arbol de Nogal**; **Ash Tree**, *Fraxinus* sp. or **Arbol de Fresno**; and **Cottonwood Tree**, *Populus angustifolia*, or **Arbol de Alamo,** are trees that are utilized, according to Doris, to regulate glucose sugar levels in the body. These trees have the qualities of being astringent or anti-inflammatory. The **Walnut tree** is also a detoxifier and cleanses the blood.

9. **Crabapple/Wild Apple**, *Malus* sp., **Manzana Silvestre**. The **Crabapple** stimulates the kidneys, allows them to function normally, and provides the appropriate energy to the body.

10. **Senna Leaves**, *Cassia acutifolio*, **Hojasen**; and **Bearberry/Buckhorn**, *Rhamnus purshiana*, **Cascara Sagrada** are used for constipation caused by lack of fiber in the diet. At the emotional level this is common with people who are inflexible and always want to be in control. Another remedy for constipation is a smoothie drink made with cucumbers, water, and a couple of ice cubes.

All of these plants are not only used and prescribed by Doris, but are part of the Mexican herbal culture. Doris prepares many of the herbs and plants described above in alcohol based tinctures which are used to prepare microdosis. Tinctures can be made with 80% alcohol, 20% water, and 200–300 grams of plant matter, while the microdosis is the opposite: a mixture made with 80% water and 20% tincture, referred to as "Mother Tincture."

The dosage of the tincture or micro dosage depends on the seriousness of the illness and varies from taking five to ten drops with water or under the tongue, every two hours to every 12 hours. Herbalists claim that five drops of a microdosis is the same as one cup of tea.

Other ways of preparing these plants are as salves or ointments or elixirs or tonics. Some of these plants can also be added to white or red wines for two weeks and consumed before or after each meal.

## 2.3 MEDICINAL PLANTS FOR THE NERVOUS SYSTEM

Leticia Amaro Velázquez, known as Lety, was another one of my brilliant teachers. She is an instructor at the famous holistic medicine school, Centro de Desarrollo Humano Hacia la Comunidad (CEDEHC) or "Center for Community Human Development" in Cuernavaca, Morelos, Mexico. Lety practices and teaches traditional massage, energetic body cleansings, Mayan acupuncture, preparation of traditional plants, and other modalities of healing. In this section, I will describe her study and practice of remedies and plants for the nervous system, which is connected to all of the other systems of the body such as the digestive, circulatory, respiratory, and reproductive systems. The nervous system is our human computer and transmits signals throughout the body. According to Lety, "Everything starts with our brain and our emotions are important to what happens with our nervous system. And that's why we need to program it with positive thoughts and actions. Instead of saying, 'I'm sick,' we need to say things that fill the body with positivity such as: 'I feel good and happy because this is going to be the best day of my life.'" Lety also tells us, "Live for today, let all of your emotions flow, and embrace people by telling them that you love them, and that this is going to be the best day for your body." I admire Lety's positive thinking that programs the brain to believe in positive thoughts, which impacts our health. It is very important to maintain our physical

**Figure 2.3** Lety discusses the medicinal plants for the nervous system.

and mental health and, as Lety states, "Mother Nature gives us exceptional plants that help with the nervous system so it can continue to work the way it needs to."

In this part, Lety discusses five of her favorite plants for the nervous system: Lavender, Rose of Castille, Rosemary, Ginkgo Biloba, and Gotu Kola. If I do not add the botanical name, it is because they have been mentioned in Dr. Enos' or Doris' subchapters. I will add additional information to Lety's description of the herbs and include some of my favorite plants that impact the nervous system in item six of the following list. In addition to the plants, Lety discusses the benefits of a facial massage on the nervous system.

1.  **Lavender,** *Alucema or Lavanda.* Several usages of this plant have been described in this chapter by Dr. Enos in his discussion of "Plants of the Southwest." However, Lety utilizes this plant for insomnia and anxiety, since Lavender is a sedative and calms the nerves, especially when we have unresolved problems during the day that our mind constantly thinks about during the night and tires our body from the necessary rest that one needs.

2.  **French Castille,** *Rosa* sp., *Rosa de Castilla.* Lety believes that the rose's beauty and pleasant fragrance helps relax the body. It is believed that medieval physicians would prepare rose petals with sugar in hot water for melancholy and depression.

3.  **Rosemary,** *Romero.* This is another plant of the Southwest described by Dr. Enos. In addition to being a blood protector and regenerator, it is also a stimulant that helps with concentration. It recuperates one's energy that may be lost because of anxiety and depression. Some call it "a plant for remembrance" and medieval physicians would place it under the pillow for treating insomnia and preventing nightmares.

4.  **Ginkgo Biloba,** *G.biloba* sp. This plant is an excellent brain oxygenator that supports the cerebral brain. It is believed that this plant may help with dementia and alzheimer's since it improves the memory.

5.  **Gotu Kola,** *Centella asiatica.* This is another brain oxygenator plant that is used for nervous disorders and called a "brain tonic." It is part of India's Ayurveda plant glossary and is said to improve meditation.

6.  **Chamomile,** *M.chamomilia,* **Manzanilla; Linden Flower,** *Tilia* sp., *Flor de Tila;* **Lemon Balm or Giant Hyssop,** *Cedronella mexicana,* **Toronjil; Passion Flower,** *Passiflora* sp., **Pasiflora; Damian,** *Turnera diffusa,* **Damiana;** and **Valerian,** *Valeriana* sp., **Valeriana.** These six marvelous plants are some of my favorites and are recommended by many of the Mexican healers for the nervous system, especially for insomnia, stress, and anxiety. I have listed these plants in order of strength, with Chamomile being the weakest, to Valerian being the stronger herb, and it should be taken for short periods of time.

Another technique for alleviating insomnia recommended by Lety, is a facial massage performed by someone else or just doing it ourselves. These steps for the facial massage are a combination of my experiences and Lety's, for the best result in relieving tension. Before beginning the facial massage you can add two or three drops of Lavender oil on both wrists, gently pressing and rubbing one against the other for a minute to bring calmness to the heart and lungs. The hands are then rubbed together to warm them and create some friction, placing them about four inches in front of the face for just a moment. The next step is a scalp massage using the fingertips to make small circles around the base of the skull, sides of the head, temple area, and pressing the top of the skull. You only need a couple of drops of Lavender oil to begin the facial massage, using your thumbs and fingers on the forehead, tracing lines from the middle of the eyebrows, even gently pinching them, moving up the forehead and across toward the temples. The closed eyes can also receive a gentle massage. The fingers are used under the bottom lip and along the cheekbones softly before finishing around the ears.

The ears have important points that connect with the rest of the nervous system. Therefore, the tips of the ears are gently pulled up, back, and down. Afterward, a light massage of the neck can be effective in continuing to relieve tension. One can now return to the scalp to end this massage with a light shampoo-type massage and pressing with your thumbs on the crown of the head. You can end the scalp, facial, and neck massage by performing sweeping motions with your hands on your scalp and face in order to remove any unwanted energy. You complete the massage like you started, by rubbing your hands to create friction and warmth, placing them about four inches away from the scalp in order to giving energy from the universe to the head.

There actually is no order on how to do a scalp, facial, and neck massage. Lety always reminds me that what is important is to have the right intentions in order to help others, in relieving illnesses related to our complicated nervous system.

## 2.4 TINCTURES AND MICRODOSIS

I would like to thank my good friend and colleague, Antonette Gonzales, known as Tonita, for her contributions to this subchapter on tinctures and microdosis. Tonita will contribute to other chapters of this book. I will also offer my own research, experiences, and opinions to this and other chapters throughout the book.

Tonita studied traditional medicine in a holistic medicine school in Cuernavaca, where she received certificates in acupuncture, medicinal plants, traditional massage, temazcal, and chronic illnesses. She apprenticed with another colleague, Rita Navarete from Mexico City, who is internationally known as an excellent practitioner and teacher of traditional medicine.

Before discussing the preparation of tinctures and microdosis, Tonita gives a brief explanation of herbalism, a cross-cultural tradition that has been used since the beginning of the human race. As I mentioned earlier in this chapter, Tonita also believes that humans learned about the usage of plants for medicine by observing animals. Many of us have seen dogs and cats that are sick eating herbs and plants to help them with their illness. Most of the time, animals also seem to know which plants are poisonous and they stay away from them. Ancient cultures learned by studying the animals and seeing what plants they were eating and how it affected them. Throughout time, herbalists examined leaves and stems of plants, naming them based on structure, appearance, and grouping them into related families. They would research to see if the plants were bitter, sweet, or sour, how they affected them and in which body systems (such as digestive, nervous, or respiratory) they work best. Also, they asked if the herbs work better topically on the skin or were more effective when taken internally.

At some point, many herbalists decided that there was an advantage to using a tincture, rather than boiling water for a tea, and that the tincture is easy and convenient to use; one can carry it in a small dropper bottle in their pockets or purse. Because the liquid extract is taken under the tongue, it enters the bloodstream faster and the action within the body has a more immediate effect. However, the usage of a tincture, microdosis, or tea is a personal preference. Mother tinctures are alcohol based, with 80% alcohol and 20% water, while a microdosis is the opposite, with 80% water and 20% alcohol-based tincture.

Before beginning the preparation of the tincture, Tonita gathers her plants from her garden asking permission of the plant and praying before cutting it, since the plant absorbs our positive or negative vibrations. The scissors or knife used to cut the plants should not be the ones used to cut food or crafts, but should only be dedicated to the plants. Tonita shared a story of how the plants can absorb negative energy from a person and that is the reason she asks permission and prays to the herbs before cutting them: Tonita states, "When I was studying herbology in Mexico, there were 15 students who were in class preparing tinctures and three of us had bad experiences that day. One student had been in terrible stressful traffic, a second student had a fight with her husband, and third one had been in a car accident.

In preparing the tinctures, all three students used the same container, scissors, plants, and alcohol to prepare the exact same herbal formula. After 30 days of maceration in the preparation of the tincture, the three students who had difficult days had plant extracts that were black and spoiled." What appears to have happened with this phenomenon is that the plants absorbed the negative experiences and vibrations of the three students.

When starting the preparation of the tincture, Tonita, once more, asks the plant permission to cut the herb with scissors that are not contaminated. She has already sterilized, by boiling in water, her Mason jar and the lid that will be used for the liquid extract. The plant she will be using for the tincture is **Mugwort**. She cuts the plant with the scissors and places it in the Mason jar leaving a small space for the alcohol to completely cover the plant. She

**Figure 2.4** Tonita preparing an alcohol-based tincture with fresh plants.

then pours into the container the Mexican alcohol made with sugar cane, which is 96% proof. She leaves enough room in the container to add 20% distilled water. If one cannot find strong Mexican alcohol, vodka can be a substitute and does not have to be diluted with water since it is only 80% proof. The next step is to label the bottle with the date, name of plant, the name of the person that prepared the tincture, and a circle with a line drawn in the center of the circle. The Mason bottle with the labeled plant soaked in alcohol is covered with aluminum foil, lightly rotated daily, and placed in a cool place for 30 days. If you prepare the tincture in a full lunar cycle, the process only requires 21 days instead of 30. After the required days, the alcohol liquid is strained, added to dropper bottles, and is ready for consumption. This alcohol-based tincture has a seven to ten year life while the microdosis will last one year, if both are stored in a cool, dark place. The following are the plants Tonita used for the tincture:

1.  **Mugwor**t, *Artemisia vulgaris* or *Artemisia* sp., **Estafiate**. This herb is one of the most important plants used in Mexico and the Southwest for a number of illnesses. Tonita uses it to treat infections since it is an analgesic, antibiotic, antiviral, and anti-inflammatory. Health practitioners in Mexico have used **Mugwort** to combat the H1N1 virus. Chinese herbalist use it in a moxa, which is a stick of dried Mugwort rolled tightly, wrapped with paper, and burned near the surface of the skin to relieve pain. It is also used for painful menstrual cramps, fever, and stomach gas.

2.  **Artichoke**, Cynara scolymus, *Alcachofa*. The vegetable, artichoke, is an excellent medicinal plant to treat liver problems. It is used as a mild diuretic in certain regions of Mexico for adult onset of diabetes.

3.  **Wild Marjoram**, *Origanum vulgare*, **Oregano** is described in the first part of this chapter by Dr. Enos in the section of Plants of the Southwest. Tonita prepares a liniment of the **Oregano** plant to be used topically and not taken orally; it is especially helpful with children, to pull down a fever by rubbing the liniment on the soles of the feet. In labeling the **Oregano** liniment, you add the date and plant, but change the symbol from a circle with a line in the center to an X in order not to ingest it orally, since it is made with rubbing alcohol. **Oregano Oil** is used for respiratory ailments, sore throat, coughs, and the symptoms associated with a cold, since it has antibacterial and anti-inflammatory qualities.

4.  **Citronella**, *Cymbopogon genus*, **Rosemary**, *Rosmarinus officinalis*. A liniment spray of these two aromatic plants can be used as an excellent insect and bug repellent. Again, we should add the X on the label indicating that is not to be taken orally.

Dried plants can also be used to make tinctures and microdosis by using a coffee filter or cheesecloth in order to strain out the plant particles.

There are people who cannot consume an alcohol-based tincture and prefer to use apple cider vinegar for the tincture or a water-based microdosis. Dr. Eugenio Martínez Bravo is considered the father of the microdosis, which he developed at the University of Zacatecas, Mexico, before his death in 2003. The microdosis is prepared by using 20% of the plant tincture called "Mother Tincture" combined with 80% distilled water. Dr. Martínez Bravo discovered that this alternative treatment had no side effects and transmitted a quick response from the tongue to the brain to the body. Tonita and many of the healers from Mexico are now using the microdosis as an effective treatment for a number of illnesses.

Both tinctures and microdosis have been beneficial in treating hundreds of patients throughout Mexico and many developing Latin American countries where people do not have access to, nor can afford modern allopathic medicine. Tonita, Dr. Enos, Lety, Doris, and many other healers from Mexico and the Southwest have learned and are teaching others how to make their own medicine for minor illnesses and how to identify major sickness and to refer patients to physicians, urgent care, and emergency rooms when appropriate. Many times, it is only a matter of using common sense in treating an illness.

# CHAPTER 3

# Juice Therapy (*Jugoterapia*)

In this chapter on Juice Therapy, *Jugoterapia*, Rita Navarrete and Tonita Gonzales share a number of natural fruits, nuts, and vegetable juices that alleviate a number of illnesses. Rita has been practicing traditional healing for almost 30 years. She began her practice in Mexico City and now has two additional health clinics in Cuernavaca and Mataxhi. Her clinic and school in Mataxhi is called *La Cultura Cura*, which means "Culture Heals" and has an objective of empowering survivors of domestic violence to heal themselves and to learn to heal others. One of her comments to her patients is, "Traditional healing is not magic and I cannot heal you, but I will teach you to heal yourselves." Rita is an excellent teacher in my traditional healing classes and travels internationally offering a number of consultations, workshops, and lectures on various traditional medicine themes. She has been described as a powerful traditional healer, *curandera*; a knowledgeable sweat lodge guide, *temazcalera*; a counselor, *consejera*; a nutritionist, *nutricionista*; a traditional chiropractor, *quiropractica*; and a motivational speaker, *oradora motivadora*. Her goal is to educate others on how to bring balance to their lives, spiritually, physically, and mentally.

Juice Therapy is a method for treating disease and illness through a diet of juices made from natural fruits, vegetables, and nuts in order to restore health, rejuvenate the body, and detoxify our system by removing accumulated metabolic waste. Juicing not only treats an ailment, but also strengthens our immune system. In juicing, Rita recommends adding half a glass of water and two or three ice cubes with some optional honey to sweeten it.

The following are symptoms and illnesses that juicing heals, and organs that juicing supports:

1. **Constipation** is caused by a lack of fiber or certain medications and results in having only three days per week of dry and painful bowel movements. Rita recommends a juice of grapefruit, papaya with three of its seeds, and a teaspoon of flaxseed. All are blended with about half a glass of water and a couple of ice cubes for less than a minute, with some pulp remaining in the blender. This smoothie has excellent fiber that cleanses the intestines. Grapefruit has vitamins A and B, while papaya contains papain, an antioxidant, and flaxseed contains an Omega-3 fatty acid.

2. **Cholesterol** is a high factor for heart disease including strokes. A juice of young tender cactus called *nopalitos* can lower the LDL bad cholesterol

**Figure 3.1** Rita demonstrating a preparation for Juice Therapy to address different ailments.

and will also control the blood sugar, which impacts diabetes. Papaya and half a teaspoon of flaxseed or chia seed are added for a healthier juice. This effective juice also helps the lymphatic and circulatory systems, and its high fiber acts like a brush cleaning the intestines.

3. **Kidneys** remove waste products from the blood and balance the body fluid. A juice of pineapple, celery, parsley, and some honey make an excellent drink to strengthen and refresh the kidneys. Instead of tap water, you can drink a tea made from *jamaica*, hibiscus flowers, which is an excellent diuretic. Rita also mentions that some emotions such as fear impact our organs, weakening our kidneys.

4. **Anemia** is the result of iron or vitamin B12 deficiency and not having enough healthy blood cells or hemoglobin. In order to alleviate anemia, Rita prepares her own natural V-8 juice to support the blood cells, improve the skin tone, strengthen the body's immune system and provide chlorophyll to fight cancerous cells. This healthy juice is prepared with some lettuce, one beet leaf, broccoli leaves with one or two florets, two spinach leaves, five celery leaves, parsley, cilantro, and one tomato. The goal is to use eight different dark greens.

5. **Acid Reflux** is also called indigestion or heartburn, which causes a burning pain in the lower chest area. **Lactose Intolerance** is the inability to digest lactose, the sugar found in milk, and causes diarrhea, gas, and bloating. These two ailments are addressed by a milk substitute and nutritious juice that Rita calls *lechada*. She blends soy powder, a teaspoon of oatmeal (can substitute with amaranth or sesame seeds). For additional potassium, she adds a banana. Additional juices that should be taken first thing in the morning, especially for acid reflux, are a smoothie of carrots, potatoes, and cabbage. Rita suggests that we add raw nuts to our juices and decorate our glass with a small leaf from the vegetables used so that we can chew and taste the individual flavors of some of the natural ingredients.

6. **The Immune System** is strengthened by taking vitamin C. A juice made of oranges, mandarins, grapefruits, and apples, is high in vitamin C. This juice also supports our kidneys.

In summary, raw juices are rich in vitamins, mineral, and enzymes that strengthen our body's functions. The properties of the fruits, vegetables, and nuts, such as calcium, potassium, and silicon, help in regenerating damaged cells and speed up recovery from illnesses.

As Rita states, "Juicing is a wonderful traditional medicine, and as Hippocrates said, 'let your medicine be your food and your food be your medicine.'"

# CHAPTER 4

# Introduction to Spiritual/ Energetic Cleansings and the Evil Eye

This chapter is a general introduction to a number of different spiritual and energetic cleansings using elements such as plants, oils, incense, spiritual water, mezcal, and eggs. You will also be able to read about spiritual and energetic cleansings from other countries in part two of this book that emphasizes a global perspective of traditional medicine. You will find both the words energetic and spiritual cleansings, in addition to "limpia," used throughout these chapters, and in my opinion they have the same meaning.

Energy healings were discussed in an interview with Dr. Gary E. Schwartz, professor of psychology, medicine, neurology psychiatry, and surgery at the University of Arizona by Bottom Line/Health Magazine. Dr. Schwartz states that energy healing has scientific evidence showing that it helps relieve pain, heals wounds, and reduces stress. He mentions that in the United States the most popular forms of energy healing is the **Healing Touch** developed in 1980 and **Reiki** in 1922. This article states that even the National Institute of Health's National Center for Complementary and Alternative Medicine has supported scientific research involving energy healing and that Eastern philosophies, for years, have addressed the powers of energy treatments, calling the life force Qi in China and Prana in India. (Schwartz, 2009)

In this first subchapter, Laurencio from the state of Oaxaca, Mexico, will demonstrate a spiritual/energetic cleansing using a number of elements, as is the tradition in his state. A second similar demonstration in the third sub-chapter will be done by Velia who is from a village in the Mexican state of Morelos. She is a powerful holistic healer in her native community. The second subchapter will have Rita and Tonita performing a different and comprehensive cleansing for fright or shock, called **susto**. This demonstration will be performed on Dr. Tom Chávez, who is a professor at the University of New Mexico and a student of traditional healing. Further along, there will be another demonstration by Rita and Tonita of how incense, such as the natural copal resin, is used with a number of antique and unusual native incense burners, called *sahumerios* in Spanish or *popoxcomitl* in the Nahuatl language. The sahumerio is used in almost all limpias performed by Mexican folk healers and in ceremonies honoring the four directions, as well as Father Sky, Mother Earth, and the heart.

Traveling to other parts of the world has allowed me to research and compare the belief systems related to the evil eye, which is a belief about how the attention of others impacts our spirit and energy. I was able to learn how people of different cultures protect and heal themselves of the evil eye. I have concentrated on the spiritual and energetic cleansings related to

**Figure 4.1** (Left to right) Hamsa from Israel, Khamsa from Egypt, and *La Mano Poderosa* from Mexico, all share a similar amulet for protection. Photo by Deyanira Núñez, University of New Mexico. Courtesy of Deyanira Núñez.

the evil eye from Mexico because the healers I trained and worked with are from Mexico, but I will expand a bit based on some of my experiences elsewhere.

Generally, an amulet is an object such as a gem, seed, bracelet/necklace, charms, and pendants. used for protection from harm such as the evil eye, while a talisman is similar with more emphasis on bringing luck and benefits. People in the first three countries (Israel, Egypt, and Mexico) use the symbol of the hand for protection from the evil eye. It is interesting that these countries have three different religions but one similar belief system for *mal de ojo* or the evil eye. This hand symbol interpreted differently according to the religions of the people that use it: Judaism, Islam, and Christianity. It should be noted that other amulets/talismans are also used for protection from the evil eye.

1. **Israel** is one of my favorite countries. I visited it as a guest of the Israeli government. After touring the modern city of Tel Aviv, the historical city of Jerusalem, and the coastal city of Haifa, I ended my trip in the town of Safed located in Northern Israel, almost 10,000 feet above sea level in upper Galilee. It was here that I was invited to dinner by a gracious Israeli family. After a lively conversation during dinner and sampling the local wine, I noticed a cast-iron hand with a blue jeweled eye in the center that was hanging next to the front entry doorway. Being curious, I asked my hostess what this interesting hand represented and this was her response: "This hand is called a *Hamsa* and is for protection against the evil eye, especially for those that enter this home. The fingers represent the five books of the Torah, which are in our Hebrew scriptures and it represents the hand of Miriam, the sister of Aaron and Moses." She continued, "I'm giving this hand to you," and she gave me a wonderful gift that I still treasure.

2. **Egypt** was a country that I visited soon after my trip to Israel. I spent time in the seaport of Alexandria and the large capital city of Cairo. At the historical marketplace in Cairo, I visited a shop and I was intrigued by a blue tin hand similar to the one in Israel and I asked the shop owner, "This hand reminds me of the one in Israel, called *Hamsa*." His answer was, "This hand is also called a *Khamsa* in Egypt, and it is for protection against the evil eye, especially for those that enter my shop. The fingers represent the five virtues of our Islamic religion, which are fasting, giving charity, daily prayer, our profession of faith, and a pilgrimage to Mecca. It also represents the hand of Fatima, the daughter of Prophet Muhammad." So, I bought the hand.

3. **Mexico** is a country that I constantly visit, and it is where my roots are. After my experiences with the *Hamsa* and *Khamsa* hands in Israel and Egypt, I unwrapped some of the mementos from my late mother's altar. For days, I had been thinking of a similar tin hand she had kept on her religious altar called *La Mano Poderosa*, The Powerful Hand. And, indeed, I found the tin hand with a written description that read, "This powerful hand of God is for protection against the evil eye, mal de ojo, and it represents the five members of the Holy Family and they are Baby Jesus, Mother Mary, Father Joseph, Grandmother Anne, and Grandfather Joachim."

4. **Greece**, specifically the popular island of Rhodes, was where I spent a couple of days visiting some ruins and exploring the market square in Lardos. It was here that I observed an older lady, who I learned was a healer, performing the Greek ritual of the evil eye call *mati*. The lady was under the shade of an olive tree praying or chanting while placing her hands on the head of a beautiful girl who seemed to be about 15 years old. After the prayer, the lady and young girl starting yawning for a few seconds. The last step of the ritual was the healer performing the sign of the cross three times and making what seemed to be spitting sounds in the air another three times. Afterward, the healer hugged the young girl. This experience was the highlight of my visit to Rhodes, Greece.

5. **Spain** is where the evil eye was introduced, beginning with the conquest of Spain by the Moors of who had come from North Africa. The Moors occupied Spain for many years and brought their

belief systems, including the evil eye and spiritual/energetic cleansing, to the Spaniards who, in turn, brought them to the Americas especially Mexico, the Southwest part of the United States and most Latin American countries. I saw a number of amulets/talismans when traveling in Madrid and Valencia, Spain. I did not witness any cleansing ritual but the objects to prevent the evil eye were evident. There were amulets/talismans similar to the ones in Egypt and Greece. I saw the Khamsa hand as well as blue glass blown jewelry with the image of an eye in the center of the glass jewels. I learned, when spending a week in Valencia, Spain, that one can stare at a baby and give him or her the evil eye. The staring is called *ojear* and some attach a red ribbon to a baby in order to ward off the negative vibrations of the stare. In reality, adults do the stare involuntary and do not mean to give the baby the evil eye, but some are thought of possessing a "heavy stare."

Growing up in a small rural town in South Texas, limpias were part of my traditional healing culture. If the babies were constantly crying, irritable, and feverish, they could be suffering from the evil eye, mal de ojo, and before beginning the limpia, the mother was asked if someone had stared at the infant and failed to touch him or her. Why is this illness prevalent with infants? It is believed that their immune system is weak and they cannot protect themselves against the negative vibrations as a consequence of the stare. However, mal de ojo can also occur in older children, teenagers, and adults, but not as often. If the person staring and admiring the child touches him or her, the negative energies are neutralized and the infant will not suffer from the symptoms of mal de ojo. The belief in the evil eye and bad energies is still alive and well all over the world and has survived hundreds of years, as explained earlier in this chapter, especially in the Middle East, a place of many rituals and strong traditional beliefs, a place where many women wear the *abaya* dress to cover their entire body and a *niqab* veil to cover their face. Their belief is that if an Arab woman, with only the eyes exposed, stares at another person, especially a baby, whose immune system is weak, that infant being stared at can get the evil eye and suffer from the symptoms of diarrhea, insomnia, and irritability. How do you prevent the evil eye? You can touch the other person, especially if it is an infant, or the baby can have an amulet or talisman, such as a bracelet or necklace charm or another object to prevent it. In Mexico, many children wear a bracelet called *ojo de venado*, which is a buckeye seed adorn with red yarn. The seed resembles a deer's eye and is why it is called ojo de venado. For protection against mal de ojo, older children and adults may wear a necklace made with small natural red beans called *colorin*. In the Middle East people wear similar amulets with blue, instead of red, yarn or blue glass jewelry, to ward off the evil eye.

If a person does get the evil eye, then a spiritual or energetic cleansing is performed by rubbing an egg and praying in order for the egg to absorb the negative vibrations that are afflicting the individual. In order to cure a person of mal de ojo, a curandero, family member, or friend performs a limpia that we will learn about in the next subchapters from well-known healers curanderas(os) such as Laurencio, Velia, Rita, and Tonita. Each of these healers has a unique way to perform a limpia. There is actually no right or wrong technique to perform a cleansing and you can even do it on yourself and receive the benefits you expect. As my late colleague and curandera Elena Ávila said, "What's important in doing a cleansing is the positive intention to help someone."

## 4.1  SPIRITUAL CLEANSING WITH LAURENCIO

I met Laurencio Lopez Nuñez a few years ago in Oaxaca, Mexico. He was an instructor in a University of New Mexico class, "Introduction to Mexican Traditional Medicine," which my friend and colleague, Dr. Terry Crowe, was offering. Dr. Crowe has been a past chair of the Medical School's Department of Occupational Therapy. Some of her experience in Oaxaca had been focused on Maternal and Child Health in Oaxaca. She invited me to participate and contribute to this excellent hands-on course in one of the most traditional cities in Mexico, Oaxaca. The objective of the course was to preserve and practice

**Figure 4.2** Laurencio performs a limpia on Cheo Torres.

a rich holistic medicine tradition that addressed healing the body, mind, and spirit.

It was at this course that I met Laurencio, a humble botanist, author, herbalist, temazcalero, and curandero. Laurencio has the characteristics that remind me of my teacher and mentor, Chenchito, who is described earlier in this book. He is sincere, gentle, kind, giving, and a person you just want to be around because of his positive attitude, love, and charisma. He learned traditional healing from his grandmother who was a well-known healer and would take Laurencio as her assistant on house calls. In addition to conducting traditional sweat lodges and limpias, he works for a local nonprofit organization that supports poor communities in installing ecologically friendly latrines that promote the overall health of the community. He is a true pioneer and one of the first to organize and support community gardens fertilized by composted treated human waste. I have invited Laurencio to be part of my traditional medicine summer school.

Every curandero(a) that I know has their own technique for performing a cleansing that is referred to as a limpia. I will discuss Laurencio's comprehensive limpias using the elements of an egg, plants, water, mezcal drink, incense, and a candle. I will also comment on Laurencio's interpretation of his limpia as well as add my comments based on research and other rituals I have observed. Before beginning the limpia, the healer usually asks the person permission to perform the spiritual/energetic cleansing.

These are Laurencio's steps, and the elements he uses in performing his limpia:

1. **Plants**—Laurencio begins his limpia by taking a bundle of plants that are full of positive energy and come from Mother Earth. These are not just any plants. They are aromatic plants such as **Rosemary/*Romero*, Basil/ *Albahaca*, Lavender/*Alhucema*,** and **Sage/*Salvia*.** These plants can be combined or used by themselves. The plant is soaked in water and used to sweep the body from head to toe, including head, face, shoulders, arms, legs, and feet. When Laurencio gets to the back of the legs, he taps the bundle of herbs against the skin repeating, "Come spirit, return to your body." The belief is that the person receiving limpia has lost his or her spirit and the plants not only sweep away negative vibrations, but also help in returning the spirit back to the body. Another theory is that the plant is smoothing the energy around our body that has been damaged by a stressful and traumatic experience. The process of sweeping the body with the plants is performed on the front and back of the body. After concluding the process of brushing the whole body, Laurencio makes invocations to protect the patient's body, mind, thoughts, spirit, and heart. After the plant ritual is completed the plants are thrown away or placed on the floor by the healer and the person, who is barefoot, will be asked to stand on the plants while the ritual continues.

2. **Egg**—Why do we use an egg? Some of the interpretations are that the egg is a living cell, therefore it is being sacrificed during the ritual. Another theory is that the egg absorbs negative energy or vibrations from the body. Some believe that when the egg is broken it resembles an eye that sees and attracts negative energy. My theory on the usage of an egg is that the mere fact that you are receiving a kind and gentle body massage with the soft and cool egg from a respected healer or family member, in prayer, with possibly love ones around you that want you to get well, is enough to help in the healing process. In this second step of the limpia, Laurencio believes that the egg represents the element of wind and during the ritual of passing it throughout the body; it pulls unwanted energy and absorbs it.

He takes the egg and makes a motion of the cross on the open hands of the person, places the egg on the open hands and once again prays while placing his own hand on the egg and states that, "This egg absorbs unwanted energy and that it cleanses the mind, body, spirit, and heart of Cheo [the person receiving the limpia] and that it bring balance, harmony, and equilibrium to him." The egg is rubbed in circular motions throughout the body beginning with the head, face, arms, hands, shoulders, legs, feet, and on the front and back of the body. Afterward, Laurencio will ask the person to discard the egg by burying it outdoors or flushing down the commode.

3. **Mezcal**—This distilled alcoholic beverage is the official state drink of Oaxaca, Mexico, and comes from the agave plant. Growing up, my dad would purchase the mezcal bottle with an agave worm inside the bottle and my uncles would bet on who would wind up eating the worm. Laurencio believes that the mezcal comes from nature and is a spiritual drink. He takes some mezcal into his mouth and sprays it on the patient and continues with the back and front of the neck, on opened hands, the navel, and feet. This practice is called "breath of life." When I do a limpia, instead of using mezcal to spray the person, I prefer placing prepared scented water such as one traditionally used by healers for limpias and protection, called Florida Water. However, I also use my own prepared Rosemary or Lavender oil scented water spray.

4. **Incense Smudging**—Many cultures around the world, especially Native Americans, have burned sacred plants such as sage and sweetgrass and used its smoke for spiritual cleansings and purification healing rituals. In this fourth stage of his limpia, Laurencio burns copal resin in a sahumerio. The copal resin comes from the **copal** tree that has been used as smudging smoke for centuries beginning with Pre-Columbian Mesoamerican ceremonies, burned in Catholic churches and used in Day of the Dead, *Día de los Muertos*, ceremonies. Laurencio smudges the person by moving his incense burner with the copal resin smoke on the front and back of the body, from the head to the feet, and across the extended arms with his movements resembling a cross. During the smudging process, Laurencio continues praying for the person and asking that the copal smoke remove and cleanse the body of unwanted energy.

5. **Candle**—In the last step of Laurencio's limpia, he gives the person a small candle and while the person is holding the candle with both hands, he tells the person that the candle is a symbol of light and that it will burn and destroy any fear, anguish, sickness, and everything that is not wanted. In return, the candle will bring peace, harmony, and happiness. The candle will be burned at home, usually before going to bed. Finally, Laurencio thanks and embraces the person for allowing him to perform the limpia.

Laurencio does a comprehensive limpia, but many that I have observed and performed are shorter in time and the elements used are only plants and/or an egg. There is actually no correct way to do it, and one can be creative in performing a limpia. I have used Eastern tradition when I have done a limpia on what I believe are some blocked chakras, which prevent the flow of energy, using the chants that corresponds to each chakra in combination with sweeping the body with herbs and an egg, completing the ritual with a copal resin smoke smudging. Those receiving this cleansing have felt much better and that is the purpose of the ritual: to help others improve their lives.

## 4.2  HEALING FRIGHT AND SHOCK (SUSTO)

In this subchapter, Rita with the help of Tonita and Tom, a student of curanderismo traditional medicine, demonstrate a spiritual/energetic treatment for susto. Dr. Tom Chávez is also a professor of educational psychology at the University of New Mexico.

What is susto? In my book, *Healing with Herbs and Rituals: A Mexican Tradition*, (2006) I describe susto as "a loss of spirit or even loss of soul or shock." Sociologists sometimes refer to susto as "magical fright." I believe

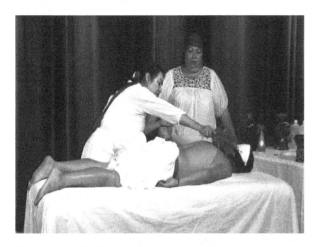

**Figure 4.3** Rita performs a limpia for susto, or magical fright, to relieve patient of negative energy.

that certain Posttraumatic Stress Disorders (PTSD) can be classified as susto since it causes stress, anxiety, flashbacks, nightmares, and uncontrollable thoughts. Rita adds to these symptoms, insomnia, lack of appetite, overeating, or suddenly jumping up from bed and not being able to go back to sleep.

What we know is that these traumatic experiences disrupt your life and interfere with your daily routine. Some of the professions in which people experience this type of trauma are soldiers returning from a war, physicians, nurses, priests, ministers, policemen, and firemen.

As a child, I experienced several sustos, and the most traumatic one was being severely mauled by a dog. In this case, my mother performed a limpia for three consecutive days: Wednesday, Thursday, and Friday. Before laying me on a warm fresh crisp white bed sheet, she blessed the bed with a knife. I then laid on the sheet and was blessed with holy water. Afterward, my mother took a bundle of sage plants and swept my body from head to toe while praying and whispering in my ear, "The spirit of Cheo, return to your body," and my answer was, "I'm coming." The belief behind reciting these words is that the traumatic experience caused your soul or spirit to leave your body, and that it can be called back. If one does not believe in the soul or spirit, we can think of our body's energy being damaged and the ritual will smooth and/or repair it. After this process was done three times, I was given a hot cup of aniseed tea, completely covered with a second warm white sheet, and by this time I was sound asleep. This ritual was repeated two more days, and then I felt much better.

Every healer/curandero has their own ritual in dealing with susto but the most important part of this procedure is the compassion, empathy, love, and affection demonstrated by the practitioner, being a healer, relative, or friend, to the person. The following is a form of limpia for susto, as performed on Tom by Rita and assisted by Tonita. This is a general outline of how one can be done:

1.  **Preparation for the Limpia**—In preparation of the limpia, Rita gathers fresh plants from Tonita's garden in order to prepare an alcohol-based maceration lotion. She prays and asks permission before cutting the following plants: **roses/*rosas,* basil/*albahaca,* rue/*ruda,* mugwort/*estafiate,* rosemary/*romero,* feverfew/*santa maria.*** All these aromatic plants are also used for several illnesses. She pulls the petals from the roses and cuts the plants with scissors dedicated only for herbs, before placing them in a large glass container with a wide opening. After the plants are in the container, she pours rubbing alcohol in order to release their properties. The alcohol completely covers the plants and the clear container is wrapped with aluminum foil (unless the container is amber colored, which has a similar function) and is kept in a cool place for two weeks with a label indicating the date and names of the plants. Before the ritual is done, the liquid is poured into an empty spray bottle. It should be noted that you can use dry plants for this preparation and the solution can also be added to an ointment or salve to massage the person. Finally, Rita gathers a bundle of the same remaining fresh herbs for a body sweep, limpia.

2.  **Limpia Face Down**—Tom is asked by Rita to lie on a massage table, face down. His body is covered with a white bed sheet that has been warming outdoors in the hot sun. Tom's eyes are also covered with a small towel, and Rita sings a soothing song to calm him. This therapy is normally done at 12 noon when the sun is at its strongest peak. Rita takes the plant prepared aromatic solution and sprays it on Tom's back and begins the massage with long strokes on Tom's body beginning with the head, to his feet, the back, shoulders, arms, hands, and legs, in order to relax the body and gain his trust and confidence. She asks Tom to remember the moment in which he suffered the susto, and reminds him to

inhale and exhale as she massages his body. Rita then takes the bundle of fresh aromatic herbs and lightly taps them against Tom's back, head, and legs as well as sweeping the body with the plants. Rita chants, "In the name of the heavens, the Earth, the four directions, may these plants remove and release your stress and emotions and return them to Mother Earth." She also asks Tom to yell his name three times in order for his spirit to return to his body. The belief is that Tom lost part of his spirit during the trauma and Rita is helping it return to his body. The concept of the susto limpia is similar to that of Laurencio's work.

3. **Smudging with Copal**—Rita takes her incense burner, adds copal, and smudges Tom's body, passing incense smoke from his head to his feet while praying and reminding Tom to relax. The copal smoke will purify and harmonize as well as cleanse any negative energy that is in the person as a consequence of the traumatic susto experience.

4. **Limpia face up**—Rita asks Tom to turn over face up. He is, once again, wrapped with the white bed sheet, his eyes are covered with a towel and the process is repeated. Tom is reminded to breathe deeply, inhaling and exhaling while thinking of his trauma and calling out his name three times in order to bring back the spirit that he's lost. Again, Rita uses the plant infused lotion to gently massage the front of Tom's body and the bundle of fresh plants is placed next to his head so that he can enjoy the fragrances before they are used to sweep the front of his body. He is once again smudged with the copal resin.

**Conclusion**—After the ritual for susto is completed, Rita gives Tom a hot cup of herbal tea to relax him. The tea could be **chamomile/*manzanilla*, linden flower/*flor de tila*, or passion flower/*pasiflora*.** She also gives Tom the bundle of herbs used in the ritual and tells him to take them and bury them in his garden in gratitude, returning them to Mother Earth.

This treatment usually takes about an hour to an hour and 30 minutes. If the trauma is serious, the ritual could be repeated three consecutive days. Some believe that susto or trauma should not be ignored but dealt with immediately, because it could turn into *susto pasado* or an old susto that is serious, and in some cases could result in death. What is important in this ritual is that loved ones, such as partners and relatives, want the person to recuperate and accompany the person who is receiving the healing. This is truly a holistic approach to healing, body, mind, and spirit.

## 4.3  SPIRITUAL CLEANSINGS WITH VELIA

Velia Herrera Arredondo comes from a small Mexican village outside of the historical town of Tepoztlan, Morelos, Mexico. Tepoztlan is considered the *Pueblo Magico* or Magical Town and is the birthplace of *Quetzalcoatl*, the serpent feathered god that was worshipped in ancient Mexico. Velia is considered the doctor of her native village, and she is an instructor at the holistic medicine school in Cuernavaca, Mexico. She specializes in a number of traditional therapies such as sobadas, medicinal plants, and limpas. In her demonstration of a limpia, she is connected to the four wind directions and to nature, especially Mother Earth. Velia's traditional limpia is described below with some additional explanations especially in regard to the four directions.

1. **Prayer/Song**—It is the custom of many native tribes to begin a ceremony or ritual with a prayer such as prayers of blessings, healing, grieving, and death. Before beginning her limpia, Velia prays and sings for her brothers and sisters who have migrated from Mexico to the United States and who are suffering, not for need of wealth, but for a lack of compassion, protection, and love. Her prayer and song is for those who are lonely and hungry and not able to grow their own food. She also prays for those who are sick and unable to receive spiritual healings.

2. **The Four Directions**—Although we refer to the four directions, many times there are actually seven. Velia places on the ground a traditional kerchief called *paliacate,* which is used in ceremonies and is also tied around the neck or covers the head. She describes the four corners of the paliacate as representing the four directions. The four directions are used in many Native American cultures with a belief that human beings are tied to all things in nature, and even to animals and colors. Each native culture has their own interpretation of the four directions and many have more than four. Velia mentions the four directions and also refers to seven. East is where the sun rises and represents a new day, new life, creation, inspiration, and originality. It represents water, and the color is yellow. The second direction is the west, where the sun sets, where you let go of things and where intuition and dreams come from. It is a place where the harvest is collected. It represents the Earth, and the color is blue or black. The third direction is south where warmth comes from and where there is a childlike place of playfulness, relaxation, and emotions. It represents fire, and the color is red. The fourth direction is north where cold and wind come from. It signifies ancestors, wisdom, and clarity. It also represents air and wind, and is associated with the color white. The fifth direction is above and is Father Sky, with the sun, clouds, rain, and the universe. It is represented by the color black. The sixth direction is below. It is Mother Earth with all the plants, rivers, animals, and humans and is connected to the color green. The seventh direction is the center and the Creator; it is also our heart, and it is associated with the color purple. Velia added other representations to some of the directions since everyone can add their own intentions to each of the directions.

3. **Popoxcomitl/Sahumerio/Incense Burner**—Velia's refers to her incense burner in her Nahuatl native language as a *popoxcomitl,* which is part of all of her healings. She adds to her popoxcomitl some hot charcoal and the sacred **copal** incense resin. Velia believes that the popoxcomitl represents the woman's womb and that the **copal** smoke is the umbilical cord that connects us to the cosmos, universe, humanity, and the Earth. She mentions the word *Ometeotl,* which is heard in most of the Mexican traditional opening ceremonies, cleansings, in traditional sweat lodges, rituals, and healings. It represents a dual cosmic energy and that we are simultaneously male and female, and invokes a balance in life of dark and light, hot and cold, and wet and dry. Velia also mentions joy and sadness, life and death, and that we are a balance of these elements in life.

4. **Smudging/Limpia**—Velia finally does a limpia on Cheryl, who works with media at the University of New Mexico. Velia asks Cheryl to face the direction of the east and uses her popoxcomitl with copal smoke to harmonize her spirit/ energy moving the incense burner to symbolize the four directions, from the head to the feet and from side to side. She moves the popoxcomitl in a half moon or a half circle and in circular motions. She is opening any energy directions that have been closed. The smudging continues to Cheryl's heart, representing the soul as well as the back of the skull, where emotions are kept, and where Velia can diagnose illnesses. In some cases, I have witnessed Velia place people into a trance if there is a trauma and if deeper spiritual healing needs to occur.

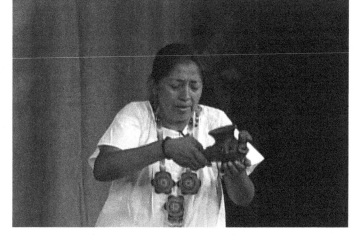

**Figure 4.4** Velia, curandera, prepares her popoxcomitl or incense burner, for her spiritual cleansing demonstration.

**Conclusion**—Velia concludes her limpia by holding Cheryl's hands in silence for a few minutes. It appears that she was transmitting positive energy to Cheryl and I could observe Cheryl's peaceful and accepting face and body language. Afterward, there was a genuine embrace by both ladies and many thanks exchanged.

This limpia was done by a person with strong native traditions. Velia has the ability, like my teacher Chenchito, to go into a trance, or perform a trance, in order to communicate with a spirit or unblock certain energies. I have observed Velia do a number of limpias and have been impressed at how she can detect people's real needs whether they are spiritual, mental, or physical.

## 4.4 BURNING INCENSE FOR HARMONIZING

Curanderos(as) such as Laurencio, Velia, and Rita have all use the traditional incense burner in their rituals. In this last subchapter, Rita and Tonita discuss the important usage of the sahumerio and perform a harmonization limpia using only the copal resin incense, on Dr. Tom Chavez. They also describe a kerchief called a paliacate, usually red color with some designs. This is a sort of table covering to place the sahumerio and copal incense on. This kerchief is also wrapped at the base of the sahumerio to protect the hands from the hot burning charcoal in the incense burner.

Many cultures use some type of incense for energetic and spiritual cleansings, as well as for harmonizing the body, whether it is with a plant, a cone or stick of incense, or a tree resin such as copal. Rita and Tonita mention the Native American use of plants for smudging such as **sage,** *Salvia apiana;* **sweetgrass,** *Hierochloe odorata;* and **cedar,** *Calocedrus decurrens.* They also discuss the use of other incense burners such as a shell or conch. Rita believes that the sahumerio represents Grandfather Fire that helps in purifying us.

Rita has an impressive collection of sahumerios from different regions of Mexico and mentions that, in her part of the country, most families in small communities have a sahumerio in their home for performing limpias, blessings, and ceremonies. I was able to learn about 12 of her antique sahumerios of different clay pigments and a number of designs. Some resemble a chalice used in a Christian Eucharist and others have a handle. Some have Aztec deities such as the Quetzalcoatl, feathered serpent god of knowledge and learning. Others have a large Aztec face or have a row of small clay skulls surrounding the incense burner. I am sure that all of them have an interesting and historical story according to the state or region they derive from. Her collection reminds me of the Pre-Columbian sahumerios on exhibit at the internationally acclaimed National Museum of Anthropology in Mexico City.

It should be noted that the collections of sahumerios used in the demonstration and video for the online class have been gifts to Tonita by different curanderas(os) from throughout Mexico. The following are the steps Rita takes in performing a harmonizing limpia with a sahumerio and copal incense:

1. **Preparing the Sahumerio**: Rita takes small pieces of *Ocote* bark, which derives from the pine tree. It is also called **fatwood** and is impregnated with terpene resin that is excellent to start fires and burns even when wet. The resin is also called *trementina* and in an ointment is used to draw out splinters. It is taken internally in small doses for chest congestion and bronchitis. The *Ocote* bark is cut into pieces measuring about 3–4 inches and placed inside the sahumerio beginning with permission to light it. The first piece of the wood is placed facing the east where the sun rises. Rita

**Figure 4.5** Rita explains the variety of incense burners used in traditional energetic cleansings and demonstrates her own type of cleansings on Tom.

continues placing the *ocote* in the positions according the other three directions, west, north, and south, resembling the ceremony of the four directions, including placing some wood in the center of the sahumerio. Once all the **Ocote** is placed inside the sahumerio, some charcoal is placed in the center and the wood is lit. Some prefer to use a round disc vegetable charcoal. The sahumerio is now ready for the **copal** incense.

2. **Copal Resin Incense:** After the sahumerio is hot, **copal** is added in preparation for the smudging. The resin of the **copal,** *Protium copal, Bursera* **spp**. is used throughout Mexico, Central, and South America for a number of ceremonies and energetic/spiritual cleansings of people or spaces. It has been used since Pre-Columbian times and the word copal, or *copalquabuitl,* derives from Nahuatl and means the "incense tree." In addition, a tea of the bark or a cold infusion of the leaves is used to treat fever and the leaves and bark, combined, are used as a tonic to strengthen the immune system. The dried **copal** can turn into an amber stone, at times with insects imbedded in the stone. I have purchased **copal** resin by the kilo at the famous Sonora Market in Mexico City and discovered that there is a brownish/yellowish copal and a white sticky copal. I prefer the white copal, which is more expensive but has a stronger and sweeter fragrance.

3. **Harmonizing Ritual:** Rita demonstrates a harmonizing ritual on Tom by first concentrating and transmitting positive vibrations to Tom. She asks him to center himself and to think positive thoughts. The belief is that the **copal** smoke is sacred and will take the positive vibrations to the heavens. Tom's aura or energy is also being cleansed in a type of limpia. Rita begins the **copal** smudging by moving the smoking sahumerio up and down and in circular movements beginning with Tom's feet and moving up to his head. This process is done on his front and back. He is reminded to continue inhaling through the nose and exhaling through the mouth. While doing the smudging, Rita, with the help of Tonita, begins to do a soothing native chant that is repeated several times with the words, "hey hey heyu wa wa."

**Conclusion:** What impressed me about Rita's harmonizing ritual was her emphasis on positive energy with the positive thoughts that she asked Tom to concentrate on. My belief is that everything is composed of energy and Rita understands this concept, especially in terms of how positive mental energy impacts the physical body. Using the sacred smoke, a soothing native chant, and positive thoughts were all part of an effective harmonizing ritual.

# CHAPTER 5
# Intestinal Blockage (*Empacho*)

I met Albertana Ortiz Nava a few years ago and realized her many talents and her impressive knowledge about traditional medicine. As with many Hispanic names, there is a shorter version or nickname for Albertana, which is "Tana." Tana has several traditional and holistic medicine diplomas in areas such as medicinal plants, traditional sobadas, oriental massage, and biomagnetism. She teaches at CEDEHC in Cuernavaca, and practices in their clinic, specializing in chronic illnesses. She has been a regular guest lecturer in my summer two-week class for about ten years and has done an excellent video on empacho for our online class.

I grew up knowing about empacho and as a young child went through the process of this treatment. This was done by my mother, who was versed in traditional medicine (especially rituals and medicinal herbs) with knowledge passed down orally from mother to daughter, as was the custom with most women in the neighborhood. My mom could not explain the things that she did because they were neither written nor were they taught in any academic program or school. Because of the oral knowledge being passed down from one generation to another, some of her traditional treatments may have been changed with time. When Tana did the video, I was able to learn that there are two types of empacho (a wet and a dry) and the proper way to massage the stomach and back of the body.

Tana explained that empacho can occur in children as well as the elderly, but it is prevalent in babies who are beginning to crawl and take things from the floor into their mouth, such as contaminated paper, plastic, or chewing gum. They may also directly swallow their food because they have not yet learned how to chew it. With the dry empacho, the symptoms are inflammation of the abdomen, watery eyes, fever, and stomach gasses without bowel movements. In the case of an infant, there is much irritability and crying with an intestinal blockage causing constipation. In a wet empacho, there is a stomach infection and diarrhea that could be caused by contaminated water or eating something from the floor that introduces unwanted bacteria to the stomach.

Tana demonstrates an empacho treatment on my friend and colleague Alex Jackson, who is a regular guest lecturer for my curanderismo classes. Alex is originally from Albuquerque, New Mexico, and is currently a practitioner of traditional medicine in Kansas City, Missouri. He specializes in Mayan abdominal massage and has trained with Rosita Arvigo in Belize, Central America, and with Rita Navarrete in Mexico City. The following are the steps that Tana demonstrates with Alex in treating empacho:

1. **Asking Permission and Connecting**: It is the practice of most healers to ask the patient for permission before performing a ritual or a healing. Therefore, Tana asks Alex if he grants her permission for the empacho treatment, and Alex responds in a positive manner. Alex is on a massage

table covered with a white bed sheet. Tana first rubs her hands to create warmth and friction and places her palms on Alex's exposed stomach for a few seconds therefore emitting her positive energy. This is a gentle touch similar to that of Reiki that utilizes touch as a universal energy for healing.

2. **Finding the Pulse**: Tana uses two techniques to determine Alex's stomach pulse: First, she places her hands on his stomach and finds his pulse. If it is superficial, strong, and sounds like running water, that is an indication that the person has empacho. The second method is for Tana to place one hand on the abdomen and with her free hand she taps on her hand, listening for the sound of a hollow drum which indicates inflammation and empacho. Both the sound of running water and that of a hollow drum are signs of empacho.

3. **Alignment of the Pulse**: Tana begins massaging the stomach in order to stimulate the intestines. She pulls and stretches the skin around the long transverse intestines where fermentation occurs and then moves to the large descending intestines where the final stage of the digestive system occurs. She moves her hands in a circular motion following the clockwise direction of the intestines. She moves to the mouth of the stomach at the base of the rib-cage and begins pulling the skin to the belly button. After she has gathered the pulse by pulling the skin, she simulates tying it into the center of the abdomen and energetically liberating it. Finally, with the tips of her fingers, Tana gently massages the stomach in circular movements and asks Alex to turn over face down. She is using massage oil and mentions that in parts of Mexico people prefer a more natural ointment call *pan-puerco* made of pig lard.

4. **Unblocking the Intestines**: In this last step of the empacho treatment, Alex is face-down and Tana will work on his back. She starts by making movements upward from the base of the spine, making small skin rolls with her fingers in order to stimulate the lateral part of the spine. With children who have empacho, one can hear soft pops while the skin is being rolled. This massage helps in stimulating and releasing the intestinal blockage. With her closed hand, she lightly taps up and down on the sides of the back and mentions that along the sides of the spinal column we have two energetic channels that connect with the intestines. Tana is stimulating and sending messages to all of the intestines and organs, therefore bringing balance to the body. She places a towel over Alex's back to avoid friction and starts pulling the towel

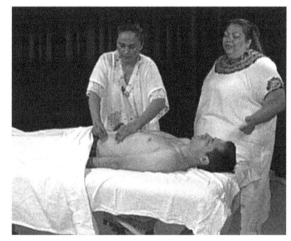

**Figure 5.1** Tana provides a demonstration of one of the techniques used for unblocking intestinal blockage, also called *empacho*.

with the skin upward from the base of the skull down the sides of the spine. If there is a popping sound while she is pulling the skin, the intestines have been unblocked. One could hear the popping sound on Alex's back indicating that he was suffering from empacho. According to Tana, if there is a popping sound on a child suffering from empacho during this stage of the treatment, they will immediately have a bowel movement. In addition to the treatment, Tana also recommends drinking fresh orange juice with a bit of olive oil to cleanse the intestines

5. **Wet Empacho**: Wet *empacho* causes diarrhea, and in children it may be the result of an intestinal parasite. Tana recommends preparing an herbal tea of **Mugwort, Estafiate, and *Artemisia vulgaris*** in order to eliminate the parasites and intestinal inflammation. Tana also recommends a diet of bland food in order to allow the intestines some time to rest. **Mugwort** is anti-inflammatory as well as excellent for the digestive system.

**Conclusion**: The treatment for empacho is still prevalent throughout Mexico, Central, and South America. If done correctly, the treatment for empacho can be effective in treating constipations as well as diarrhea. I have taken massage classes and remember my instructors stating that the parts of the body that work the hardest, such as the feet and stomach, are usually neglected in a massage. Tana's demonstration of the stomach massage is a perfect example of embracing and massaging our neglected body organs.

# CHAPTER 6
# Shawl Alignment
# (*Manteadas*)

Rita Navarrete, growing up in a small rural town a few miles outside of Mexico City, remembers neighbors and the local healer doing shawl alignments, called *manteadas*. After many years of practice and studying curanderismo, she understood the benefits of manteadas. And so she began practicing the ancient treatment using a cotton-like sheet to manipulate the body, especially with the elderly, children, and pregnant women. I asked Rita why they called this treatment manteada and she responded that it comes from the word *manta* meaning, "unbleached cotton garment" or a type of shawl. This is probably why it is translated as "shawl alignment," because women would actually use their shawls, called *rebozos*, as a healing treatment. In many parts of Mexico, Central and South America, the use of the shawl is versatile. It can be used by women to stay warm, to cover their head when attending church services, to wrap an infant, to carefully wrap a baby and carry the infant on the front or back of the body, in addition to massages.

The manteada is usually used on pregnant women, the elderly, and children. One needs to be careful in performing a massage on a pregnant woman for fear of inducing labor. If a baby is in breech, a manteada can help in turning the baby in the correct position. In a breech position, the baby's bottom or feet are first instead of the child being in a head down position and if this is not corrected, the result could be serious injury or even death. With a special massage and gentle manteada with rocking movements, the infant's body can be rotated to be in the correct birthing position. Other issues that can be alleviated with a manteada are sciatica pain, spinal alignment, and postpartum disorders such as closing the hips called *cerrando la cadera*.

The elderly are a second group that can benefit from a manteada. A gentle geriatric massage combined with a manteada can help with depression, improve balancing, add flexibility, and help with a better posture. It can also reduce pain, especially from arthritis, and increase the circulation of blood.

With children, a light massage followed by the gentle manteada rocking, calms them down, helps with anxiety, and promotes sleep.

Rita, with the help of Tonita Gonzales, demonstrates a manteada treatment on a student of traditional medicine and nurse, Katalina Gurule, known as Kata. The following are the steps that Rita, with some help from Tonita, takes in demonstrating a manteada on Kata;

1. **Preparation for the *manteada***: Rita emphasizes that, before the manteada treatment, her muscles should be stretched in order to protect herself and she begins a five minute warm-up exercise. In a standing and comfortable position, she rotates and moves her shoulders, wrists, legs, feet, and waist. She takes an unbleached cotton sheet called a *manta* and makes sure that Kata will lie on the center of the sheet, which is on the floor, and that each end of the sheet is equal. Kata lies on the center of the sheet and Rita takes an ointment of hot plants that she has previously prepared. Most of the hot plants she recommends for this ointment have already been discussed in the medicinal plant chapter of this book and they are **Rosemary, Aloe Vera, Eucalyptus, Golden Root, Feverfew,** and **Mugwort.** In

order to warm Kata's muscles, hydrate her skin, and relax the body, Rita takes the oil and massages it on her neck, the fourth and fifth lumbar region where there is usually pain, on the feet, shins, legs, and lightly on the knees.

2. **Performing the Manteada**: During the manteada, it is not necessary to remove one's clothing. Rita begins by asking Kata to remain lying on her back on the cotton sheet, which is on the floor. She covers Kata's eyes with a small cotton cloth and stands with each foot next to the center of Kata's body. Looking at her lying on the sheet, she reminds Kata to continue breathing by inhaling and exhaling. She takes both ends of the sheet wraps them around her hands and begins pulling

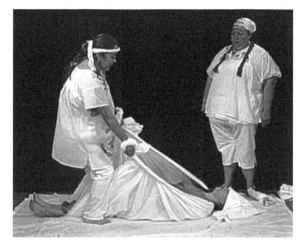

**Figure 6.1** Rita performs a gentle *manteada*, or shawl alignment, to alleviate muscle discomfort.

each side of the sheet, rocking Kata from side to side, creating a soothing massage. She pulls one side of the sheet, rocking the shoulder that was previously massaged with hot oils, creating a deeper massage. Rita continues reminding Kata to continue breathing by inhaling and exhaling in rhythm to the movement of the sheet. She is still standing over Kata, holding the ends of the sheet and rocking the gluteal muscle area by moving the sheet back and forth and side to side. This process is done on the neck, on the legs and feet. After the rocking motion, the sheet is pulled tightly on Kata's body and tucked in place. Kata is now looking like a wrapped mummy, but feeling nurtured and loved.

3. **Performing a Manteada with Two People**: Rita, with the help of Tonita, briefly demonstrates a manteada done with two people. Each takes one end of the sheet and rocks Kata's body, crisscrossing the sheet by taking the opposite ends and pulling on the sheet in order to create a tight fit on Kata's body. Both ends of the sheet are again tucked in place. Rita reminds us that two people doing the manteada on a heavy person is preferred in order to prevent any injury.

**Conclusion**: Even though the healing method of the *manteada* has been around for many years, it has made a comeback and the technique appears to be improving since it is now being taught at holistic naturopathic schools in Mexico. I am amazed at how it is serving a population in our society that many times are neglected, such as pregnant women, the elderly, and children. This technique offers a gentle caress to the soul and body. There is a term that is common in Mexico for this: *apapacho*.

# CHAPTER 7

# Introduction to Healing with Fire, Earth, and Oils

This chapter of healing with fire, earth, and oils will offer three traditional healing modalities that were used in earlier times and have resurfaced. The usage of fire cupping is called *ventosas*, and I have heard a number of stories of how mothers and grandmothers were using this healing method in earlier years with a simple method and not as comprehensively as my colleague Rita will demonstrate in the following subchapter.

The ancient practice of cupping is practiced all over the world, especially in Europe, Asia, and Africa. It has been mentioned in one of the oldest Egyptian medical textbooks, the Eber Papyrus (Saber, 2010). When we hear the word "cupping," some believe that it originated in China and may not realize that fire cupping has also been used for hundreds of years in Mesoamerica.

I remember watching the Olympics on television and seeing Michael Phelps with purple bruises on his back as he won his 19th Gold Medal at the 2016 Summer Olympics in Rio de Janeiro, Brazil. Because of the marks, I immediately realized that he had gone through a Chinese cupping treatment since Mexican running cupping (see below) usually does not leave bruising marks. The reason for his cupping session was that he probably was suffering from sore and overworked muscles that needed to be loosened. If Michael was treated by Rita, his bruising would not have been evident since the running cupping would not leave marks on his back. I believe that the recent usage of cupping by Michael Phelps and other Olympians has made this treatment more popular than ever. Many are now asking about its benefits including how this deep tissue massage relieves pain, reduces inflammation, promotes blood flow, dispels stagnant blood, and helps the lymph nodes.

There are basically three methods of cupping: dry, wet, and fire cupping. Dry cupping involves creating low air pressure on the skin by heating a cup with an open flame and placing it on the skin in order to pull the skin. This air vacuum can also be created by a mechanical suction rubber cup that is left in place for a few minutes, creating skin markings. The wet cupping process is similar but is usually done in a sauna with mechanical valves and is practiced in northern European countries such as Finland, in some Indigenous cultures, and Muslim countries, where cattle horns with smoothed edges are sometimes used. It often draws blood. Finally, the fire cupping is the process that Rita does with the flame of a cotton ball placed on a glass cup in order to pull up the skin. In this process, oil is applied to the body in order for the cup to glide over the muscles. Additional information on fire cupping as performed by Rita is provided in the following subchapter.

The second subchapter discusses healing with the earth, which we refer to as Geotherapy. Tonita demonstrates the usage of clay and some plants as a healing therapy. Friends have shared with me stories of how their ancestors would dig certain types of earthen clay, soften it with a medicinal herbal tea, and place the mud on parts of the body afflicted with pain associated with arthritis, rheumatism, or a sprain. If they lived in an isolated farm or ranch area, the local huesero/bonesetter, or a family member could prepare a clay cast for broken bones.

In the last subchapter, Rita demonstrates the use of herbal oils on the back, especially the spinal column, to assist in a number of ailments. She begins by using a brush to stimulate and open the skin pores on the back of the body, in order to prepare it for the use of herbal oils that penetrate the skin and support some neuromuscular disorders.

## 7.1  FIRE CUPPING (*VENTOSA*)

Rita begins her demonstration of fire cupping by naming the materials she uses in performing a ventosa or fire cupping. Both words, ventosa and fire cupping, have the same meaning, and I will be using the terms interchangeably in this chapter. She mentions using thick glass tumblers, empty baby Gerber jars, and special Chinese cupping glasses of various sizes to adapt to different parts of the body. She discussed the use of locking hemostats to clamp the alcohol dampened cotton balls with 99% Isopropyl rubbing alcohol, a lighter or matches, and a glass of water, to deposit the used cotton balls. She also uses a face towel to wipe the excess alcohol from the ventosa glasses, and three spray bottles. The first bottle contains alcohol to spray inside the ventosa glass, to create more pressure for a deeper tissue cupping. The second spray bottle has massage oil and the third one contains herbal oil. Finally, there is an ointment that Rita has prepared using 18 hot plants for massaging before and after the treatment, to better move the *ventosa* glass and to allow the plant essence to help with any muscular pain. Rita is an expert at performing fire cupping and has more material than others may use for a basic ventosa.

1. **Preparing for the Ventosa**: After placing all of the material mentioned next to the massage table where the ventosa will take place, Rita reminds us that one should be confident and sure of performing this method and that we should touch the body with respect, tenderness, and love, and concentrate on the needs of the person receiving the treatment. The healer should prepare for the treatment by maintaining proper posture, breathing correctly with constant inhaling and exhaling, and the leg movements should be relaxed and flow as if dancing.

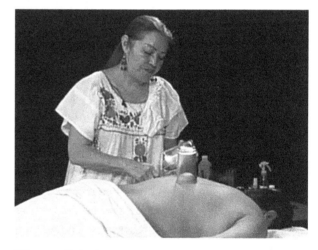

**Figure 7.1** Rita provides a demonstration of fire cupping, using two glasses, which can alleviate muscle pain and increase blood circulation.

2. **Ventosa on the Back**: Rita uses a hemostat to grab a cotton ball that has been soaked in rubbing alcohol and lights it with a candle. With the hemostat, she lights and places an alcohol soaked cotton ball under a *ventosa* glass and quickly puts it on the back of the patient next to the spinal column. Immediately, she repeats this process with a second glass, places it opposite the first one and quickly pulls the first glass. She repeats the process, with two glasses on each side of the spinal column up and down the back. The fire inside the two glasses is creating a suction that is pulling the skin. After this process is done two or three times, Rita massages the entire back with an ointment she has prepared with hot plants. Again she begins a similar process but this time she sprays alcohol inside the glass for a stronger pressure and allows the glass to glide over the muscle groups in a running cupping/*ventosa corrida* technique. Finally, she uses a smaller glass to do a ventosa on the neck area using a zigzag movement.

3. **Ventosas for Sciatica**: The sciatica nerve pain is fairly common and runs from the lower back to the buttocks and legs. Rita demonstrates the usage of ventosas to treat sciatica by beginning the ventosas on the gluteus maximus muscle located on the buttock and moving down the leg to the foot, where smaller suction glasses are used. Afterward, she lubricates the same area with an ointment and does the running ventosas in a zigzag motion. She completes the process with a general soothing massage.

4. **Ventosa for a Dislocated Wrist**: For a dislocated wrist, Rita does a treatment on the hand, wrist, and arm. Using a herbal oil, she massages the entire arm beginning with the fingers of the hand. It is visible that there is a better blood circulation on the arm, wrist, and hands since the skin is turning a reddish color. After she has warmed the area with the ventosa and a soothing massage, she ties a kerchief around the wrist and manipulates the arm by pulling on the wrist in different directions until she has readjusted the muscles in the correct position.

5. **Postpartum Ventosa**: Many times there is stomach inflammation and pain after childbirth. After several years of doing postpartum treatments, Rita has discovered that ventosa can be helpful in expelling trapped air and gasses after cesarean childbirth. She begins this process by doing ventosa on the stomach in a circular motion, using hot herbal oils for a gentle stomach massage in a circular movement. She completes the treatment with a compress of fresh hot plants by placing them on the stomach in order to relieve inflammation and pain. This treatment also helps in closing the hips.

**Conclusion**: I have not found many scientific studies and evidence that proves the effectiveness of ventosa; however, Rita can tell many stories of how hundreds of her patients have felt relief, after a fire cupping session from a number of ailments, including pain and stress. I can testify that after several years, my chronic sciatica was cured with a couple of intensive ventosa sessions.

## 7.2 GEOTHERAPY

In this subchapter, Tonita discusses the wonders of nature and how we can use the clay of the earth to heal and keep us healthy. The therapeutic method of using clay is called Geotherapy. In this process, the clay cools the body heat that is causing inflammations, discomfort, and internal fevers. Tonita briefly shares with us a related therapy called Thalassotherapy based on the usage of seawater and sea products like sand. This healing technique involves burying the patient in beach sand that is three feet deep, with only the neck and face exposed, and with a shade protecting the face from the sun. This treatment is effective in pulling uric acid from the body and can change the pH (potential hydrogen) balance of acidity and alkalinity.

The usage of Geotherapy is excellent in removing hot ailments from the body and bringing it into balance and in addressing infections, inflammations, and toxins. Tonita connects the use of clay to the hot and cold theories of the humors, which teaches that the body should have a balance of hot and cold temperatures and that when the body is not in balance, we get sick. We learn from the animals that cover themselves with dust or mud in order to feel better. Clay may contain a number of minerals

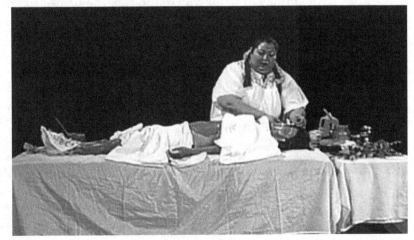

**Figure 7.2** Tonita provides a demonstration on clay therapy and lettuce to reduce inflammation and treat skin problems.

that can impact the body such as iron, zinc aluminum, calcium, sodium, and potassium and, in combination with herbal teas or fresh plants, can provide nourishment to the cells.

Collecting the clay is important in order to keep it as pure as possible. Tonita recommends that we find a noncontaminated area where one can dig a hole at least three feet deep, since natural deposits and minerals can filter bacteria at this depth. Outside of Albuquerque, Tonita finds rich red clay at some of the mountain areas around the Jemez region. She recommends mixing the clay with an herbal tea and placing it on the body for about 45 minutes to an hour, for the best results.

Some of the medicinal plants that are added to the clay for a number of ailments are the following:

1. **Clay with *Yerba Mansa***: Dr. Enos describes **Swamp Root**, *Anemopsis, **Yerba Mansa**/**Bavisa** in an earlier chapter "Plants of the Southwest" as an excellent herb for reducing inflammation. Boiled as a tea and mixed with the clay it is used to treat skin infections, skin bacteria, acne, and inflammation. It can be applied directly to the skin or on top of a gauze since the holes on this cloth can allow the clay to breathe. The clay mixture should be allowed to dry in order for it to soak completely into the skin.

2. **Clay with French Rose and Chamomile**: In the earlier chapter on "Plants for the Nervous System," Lety describes **French Rose**, *Rosa* sp., ***Rosa de Castilla*** and **Chamomile**, *M.chamomilla*, ***Manzanilla*** as plants for relaxation. However, Tonita also recommends that the tea from both plants can relieve eye irritations by placing a leaf of lettuce over the eye and adding a thin layer of clay on top of the lettuce that has been mixed with either plant.

3. **Clay with Lettuce**: Tonita recommends that **lettuce** can replace gauze on just about any part of the body and should be covered with clay. **Lettuce**, *Lactuca sativa*, is anti-inflammatory and contains several minerals and vitamins such as calcium, iron, and potassium. She suggests that **lettuce** covered with clay be mixed with an herbal tea or fresh cut-up plants, such as **Mugwort/*Estafiate*** or **Rosemary/*Romero.*** This can be used on most parts of the body or the clay can be placed directly on the skin without the lettuce. One important area of the body is the abdomen, when a healer wants to cool the body and reduce a fever, especially with children. With women, it supports them through hot menopausal flashes and on the feet it reduces inflammation, especially with gout. The clay mixture on top of the **lettuce** can be applied thicker on the feet. A strong **lettuce** tea, without the clay, can be used in a warm bath to help with inflammations.

4. **Clay with Onion Skin**: The thin **onion** skin can be peeled and, like the **lettuce**, can be placed directly on skin infections and covered with clay mixed with ***Yerba Mansa***. The **onion** skin is an antioxidant, is anti-inflammatory, and helps in healing scars.

5. **Clay with Marigolds**: The use of **Marigolds** is discussed by Doris in the chapter "Medicinal Plants for the Digestive System." Tonita recommends that the **Marigold** flowers can be chopped and added directly to the clay mixture, and used for skin problems, such as psoriasis, eczema, and other skin allergies and irritations.

**Conclusion**: Mother Nature offers us earth to heal through Geotherapy with the mixture of medicinal plants. In addition to mixing medicinal herbs with the clay, one can substitute cornmeal, which is also natural and effective. Geotherapy is a healing modality that anyone can use with clay from their backyard and plants from their gardens. Tonita demonstrates this free and easy natural healing technique that has been used worldwide for thousands of years. Many people have now rediscovered the simple and effective way to empower ourselves and to address many of our maladies. Children enjoy playing with mud, can become excellent healers using Geotherapy on themselves or others, and can rinse themselves outdoors using a water hose. What an effective way to maintain good health and have fun at the same time.

## 7.3 HEALING WITH HERBAL OIL

I am thankful that Rita has shared her wisdom and knowledge with us in demonstrating a number of traditional healing modalities. In this subchapter, she describes and demonstrates the use of certain oils with a gentle massage that stimulate the spinal column, also referred as the spinal cord or the backbone. It is composed of nerve tissues that, with the brain, make up the central nervous system.

Before beginning her demonstration with oils, she mentions that her treatment addresses some relief for sclerosis, which is hardening of the body tissue. This may have a negative effect on the nervous system. She mentions that back pain can be caused by damaged spinal discs that are ruptured or herniated as a result of age, disease, or injury. Other pain could be related to constantly being in the same body position, such as constant work with a computer for a length of time or continuously walking incorrectly. Because chiropractic manipulation may not be possible, this becomes a gentle treatment where Rita is careful in not creating additional injury to the spinal column. She begins by placing herbal oil at the cervical spine of the neck and moving to the lumbar region of the lower back.

The application of oils to the body has been used for generations by many cultures since they are quickly absorbed by the skin for nourishing and healing purposes. The following are the steps Rita takes in her demonstration, using herbal oils on Tom Chávez with the assistance of Tonita Gonzales:

1.  **Preparation for the Oil Treatment**: Rita prepares the materials to be used in this treatment, including a soft body brush, salt, and an oil prepared with hot plants, to be used as an analgesic to relieve pain. She has an additional plant-based oil for a gentle massage to relax the back, a small cotton body towel to cover the back, and hot salty water.

2.  **Usage of the Brush**: Tom is asked to remove his shirt and sit face-down on a chair massage table such as the ones seen at airports and shopping malls, available for about a 15-minute back massage. Rita takes the body brush and begins brushing Tom's back from the lower back up the neck area with gentle brush strokes from the spinal column out to the rib cage. After the brushing is done a few times, she taps the brush bristles on Tom's back a few times. The purpose of the brushing and tapping is to release dead skin cells, open the skin pores, and stimulate the millions of nerve cell neurons. After this process is done a few times, Rita observes that Tom's back is turning a reddish color indicating that the skin pores are waking up and almost ready to accept the herbal oil.

3.  **Hot Towel Salt Water Compresses**: Rita prepares a hot towel salt water compress by placing a body towel that has soaked in a mixture, squeezing it and places it over Tom's entire back. With the palms of her hand she lightly presses on top of the towel and throughout Tom's back allowing skin pores to continue opening and absorbing the salt water, which has anti-inflammatory qualities. She repeats the process of pressing on the back, the neck area, the shoulders, and the lower back.

4.  **Oil Drops on the Back**: By this time, the constant brushing and hot salt water compresses have completely opened the body's pores and Tom's back is ready to accept the herbal oil. The oil is prepared with hot plants, which include: **Oregano, Rue, Feverfew, Eucalyptus, Malabar, and Aloe Vera**. Rita places about a drop of oil

**Figure 7.3** Drops of certain oils can be used on the spinal column as a gentle therapy, as Rita demonstrates in the image.

per inch throughout Tom's back and allows the oil to run down the back, especially on the spinal column. She lightly spreads the oil with the tips of her fingers and you can actually see the oil penetrating the skin and can smell the pleasant aroma of the plants. She completes the treatment by a using additional oil for a very gentle and kind massage throughout the back, neck, and shoulders, reminding Tom to continue breathing by deeply inhaling and exhaling.

**Conclusion:** I am impressed with the gentle and kind therapeutic treatment that Rita uses in dealing with a sensitive part of the body, the spinal column. Most of the treatment is preparing the body with constant brushing of the skin and using a hot salt water compress in order to completely open the skin pores and accept the herbal oil. In preparing the skin, Rita could actually see the opened pores quickly absorb the herbal oils, whose pleasant aroma was also part of the aromatherapy treatment.

# CHAPTER 8
# Temazcal

## 8.1 THE NATIVE AMERICAN SWEAT LODGE

It was almost 20 years ago that I experienced my first sweat lodge. A colleague, the late Arturo Sierra, invited me to join him in a Lakota sweat lodge that he also referred to as an *Inipi* purification ceremony. But he told me very little about the experience. He did say to eat lightly and to take shorts, a towel, and some tobacco as an offering. I had heard the term "sweat lodge" but knew nothing about this Native American tradition nor had I heard of the word temazcal, for a Mexican sweat lodge.

When I arrived to our host's home, I followed a group of mostly Native American men of different tribal affiliations to the backyard where I saw a dome-shaped, igloo-like structure covered with a blanket. A short distance from the small front door opening of the lodge was an open fire in a pit heating a number of large volcanic rocks. I introduced myself to the group and met the sweat lodge elder to whom I gave the tobacco gift offering. Before entering the sweat lodge, I joined the group of about 10 men who formed a circle and were all smudged with the sage plant and fanned with an eagle feather, as the elder leader sang a native song to the beat of a drum. The pleasant smell of the sage, the hypnotic chant, and the warmth of the fire heating the rocks immediately calmed my nerves. Before entering the lodge, we all bowed to the Great Spirit and to Mother Earth as we got on our knees to enter the small opening in the lodge and continued crawling clockwise until we found our place, forming a circle. As we sat on the ground with our legs crossed, staring at a shallow pit in the center of the lodge, the sweat leader called for a man outside, called a doorkeeper, to drop a canvas flap covering the lodge door opening and converting the dimly lit lodge into a totally dark place. The sweat guide introduced himself and said that anyone is free to leave if they were not ready for the experience, and no one left.

After a short prayer in his native language, he asked the doorkeeper to open the flap and to bring the heated stones from the burning fire. About 10 red hot stones were brought in a shovel and placed in the pit inside the lodge, a few inches in front of the group, and I immediately felt the strong heat. The door flap was closed and the lodge guide took water in a dipper from a pail next to him and poured it on the rocks, producing a very hot steam. I immediately placed a wet face towel on my face praying that I could endure the experience. After some chanting and motivating comments by the sweat guide and others, that lasted about 20 minutes, the door flap was lifted and the outside cool air was a welcome feeling. This first session was called a round, and I was to experience two more rounds with additional hot rocks for each round, totaling about 30 red hot stones. Each round was different, with chanting, drumming, and passing the peace pipe. After an hour experience inside the lodge, we left the lodge crawling out left to right, dried our bodies of all the sweat, and were invited to our host's home to enjoy a light snack of soup, vegetables, and fruit. After going home, bathing in a warm shower, I slept like a rock, enjoying some sweet dreams. I could not believe how energetic I was all that week and was looking forward to the next sweat. I experienced several other sweat lodges and later noticed that a few feet from the men's lodge was a women's lodge, with many of the ladies being wives or partners to the men.

## 8.2 THE TEMAZCAL EXPERIENCE IN MEXICO

A few years later, I visited my colleague, Dr. Arturo Ornelas, in Cuernavaca, and was invited to his temazcal sweat lodge, something somewhat different than the Lakota one. Arturo's temazcal is part of his teaching curriculum at his holistic school of traditional medicine called *Centro de Desarrollo Humano Hacia la Comunidad*, Community Human Development Center. He and some of his instructors, participate in the annual two-week class and the semester-long online course that I teach at the University of New Mexico. Arturo's invitation to his temazcal was a blessing, since I was suffering excruciating pain from a chronic sciatica problem I had suffered for years. The pain would flare-up after running or walking on a hard surface for a length of time, and I did my share of walking in Mexico City and Cuernavaca. I shared this problem with Arturo, and he suggested I start relaxing my muscles in the temazcal, followed by a special cupping ventosa treatment. This temazcal was different than the Lakota sweat lodge experience.

The structure was a permanent circular dome and appeared to be constructed with volcanic rock and cement. The opening was larger than the Lakota one and the floor was concrete, covered by a mat called *petate*, which is made of the woven fibers of palm leaves. On top of the mat were aromatic plants that seemed to be Basil combined with Rosemary and both produced a sweet and powerful fragrance. There was no ceremony before entering the temazcal and the group was about six people, including Arturo, his wife, and daughter. The volcanic rocks heating the temazcal were not in the center of the lodge but were in a firebox on the west side of the structure and opposite to the east door entrance. They were being heated by wood at an outside opening of the firebox that had been burning for several hours. There was a large brown clay pot with a fragrant tea that produced a sweet minty smell when poured with a dipper on top of the hot rocks. The steam was hot but at a lower temperature than a Lakota sweat, reminding me that this was a more therapeutic experience than ceremonial. Arturo did chant some soothing *Nahuatl* songs and asked the group to join him.

After about 40 minutes and a good sweat, I was wrapped in a wool blanket and asked to lie on a mat and covered with another blanket. Then I was given a cup of a delicious herbal tea and asked to rest. I immediately went to sleep and was woken up about an hour later by a healer who later became a dear friend and colleague, Rita Navarrete. Rita was targeting my sciatica problem so she performed a deep tissue massage, pulled my leg, kneaded my gluteus maximus, pressing on my thighs and hamstrings, and worked her way to my feet. After about an hour of an intensive massage, I was given another cup of herb tea and took another nap that resulted in sleeping throughout the night and waking up early the next morning full of energy and completely pain free.

Soon after this experience, I joined my colleague Dr. Terry Crowe, professor of Occupational Therapy, on a trip with a group of university students to Oaxaca, Mexico, where I experienced my second temazcal with Laurencio Nuñez. This experience was near the small beach town of Mazunte, Oaxaca, with lots of remote natural surroundings. After the students and I received a spiritual limpia cleansing, we entered the temazcal, which was located on the beach, with a relaxing sound of the ocean waves and a soothing cool moist sea wind. This experience was memorable and extremely therapeutic.

After visiting with Laurencio, I discovered that the usage of the temazcal is still popular in the state of Oaxaca and is used for birthing, postpartum healing, marriage ceremonies, for detoxification, and family events. In some homes, the temazcal is part of the daily life, is attached to the home, and you can enter from the living room or one of the bedrooms.

## 8.3 THE TEMAZCALS IN NEW MEXICO

After my experiences with the temazcals in Cuernavaca and Oaxaca, Mexico, I learned that the origin of this pre-Hispanic Mesoamerican tradition is traced to the Aztec culture and that temazcal comes from the Nahuatl word temazcalli meaning house of vapor/heat with "*tema*" meaning vapor, and "*calli*" meaning house. There are many similarities between the Native American sweat lodge and the Mexican temazcal, such as it being a place of purifying and cleansing body, mind, and spirit.

Just as there has been a renewed interest in reviving the temazcal culture in Mexico, New Mexicans have also begun constructing temazcals in the Albuquerque area. The first temazcal built by a curandero from Mexico was commissioned by the late Ben Tafoya, director of Hoy Recovery Program, Inc. who decided to build two temazcals, one for men and the second one for women, in a small community located in northern New Mexico. Hoy Recovery Program is a drug and alcohol rehabilitation center that provides short- and long-term treatment for substance abuse, including detoxification. Mr. Tafoya asked a curandero from Mexico, Roberto, to construct the temazcals and invited some of the healers from Mexico to come on a monthly basis and conduct the temazcal ceremonies with clients at the recovery center. This program proved to be effective in addressing detoxifications as well as an opportunity to discuss, in the temazcal, problems and solutions that led the person to substance abuse.

The second one was built by my colleague and spiritual healer, Laura Alonzo de Franklin. Laura is a founder of *Kalpulli Teocalli Ollin*, (Community Sacred House of Healing). Laura began her healing path learning from her mother and maternal grandmother in Mexico and South Texas. She has used her traditional healing in helping the community, especially veterans. A few years ago, she invited Roberto to help build a temazcal named *Temazcalli Teocalli Ollin* in her backyard in Los Lunas, a few miles from Albuquerque. She invites my students in the two-week summer curanderismo class to experience her temazcal, and offers different types of options such as the following:

1. **Honoring the Light Warrior Within, through MesoAmerican Indigenous Positions**: This temazcal involves breathing, body movements, hand and feet placements, and other techniques that connect and guide us along our ancestral spiritual path with love and light. It is for men and women.

2. **Female Archetypes of the Mexika Medicine Wheel and Connecting the Temazcal through Aromatherapy**: The experience is to enter the sacred womb (the temazcal lodge) and experience a MesoAmerican temazcal ceremony around archetypes using essential oils, meditation, song, and coming full circle within the *Mexika* medicine wheel. This temazcal is only for women.

3. **Connecting the Body, Mind, and Emotions**: This men and women's temazcal involves healing through hands-on *sobadas* (traditional massage).

4. **Instructional and Experiential Temazcal**: This session combines instruction on how to conduct and lead a temazcal ceremony with going through an actual experience lead by the temazcalero (specialist in temazcals) Laurencio Nuñez.

After the construction of the two temazcals in Alcalde and one in Los Lunas, New Mexico, Tonita Gonzales began construction of a temazcal in the North Valley of Albuquerque. This temazcal was designed by Rita and constructed by Tonita's father, who is the owner of a construction company. He used quality material such as fire resistant brick, drainage, and propane gas, for quick heating of the rocks. It has a bench that encircles the inside of the lodge, making it accessible to people of all abilities, especially to accommodate those with knee problems and the elderly that cannot sit on the floor. Tonita has offered her temazcal to hundreds of groups and community members.

She has also invited students in my two-week curanderismo summer class to experience the temazcal and offers the following themes:

**Figure 8.1** Traditional Mexican Temazcals, or sweat lodges, vary in size and can accommodate different group sizes. Tonita's temazcal (above) can serve up to 20 individuals.

## 8.4 FOR MEN AND WOMEN

1. **Temazcal de Barro (Clay):** The combination of cleansing with clay (Geotherapy), song, and prayer, detoxifies the body, mind, and spirit. A full clay body mask prepared with medicinal teas will allow for a deep cleansing.

2. **Temazcal for Healing Emotions in the Sacred Womb:** This experience is a re-entering the womb (the temazcal is considered the womb of Mother Earth) allowing us to sit in the darkness of which we were born to focus on ourselves and begin to confront our emotions, voice them, and heal them through song and sound.

3. **Temazcal Dulce (Sweet Temazcal):** Experience a bed of the Basil herb, a sacred euphoric plant that helps heal emotions and is also for infertility issues and postpartum depression.

4. **Healing our Breath:** Indigenous medicine teaches that our breath supports the healing of our grief and sadness, which is addressed in this temazcal, as well as dealing with respiratory illnesses.

### For Women

1. **Temazcal of Sacred Cacao (Chocolate) and Sacred Blue Corn:** This traditional sacred ceremony honors the divine feminine with the usage of southern cacao and northern blue corn as used in the Mexican and Native American traditions. Women receive a full body mask using the sacred formula to promote the healing of the divine feminine body, in addition to a special herbal tea.

2. **Temazcal of Rosas y Miel (Roses and Honey):** You experience the healing properties of washing the body with sacred honey and adoring the body with kisses of fresh rose petals.

### For Men

1. **Warrior Temazcal:** Through song, prayer, and ceremony the men come together to begin the day with intentions of healing themselves and the community.

*Temazcal Tonantzin* is the name Tonita has given her temazcal with the Nahuatl word *tonantzin* meaning "Our Sacred Mother," symbolizing the earth and fertility. Some refer to the Virgin of Guadalupe as *Tonantzin* Guadalupe. Tonita also requests the students to notify her of health conditions before entering the temazcal, such as high blood pressure or pregnancy. Drugs and alcohol are prohibited. She recommends a light and nutritious meal one to two hours before entering the temazcal.

## 8.5 A TEMAZCAL EXPERIENCE BY RITA NAVARRETE

Rita conducts a number of temazcals at her clinic in Mexico City and the sweat lodge structure is indoors, adjoining her home. She also has two temazcals in other Mexican communities and teaches classes on building and conducting the various temazcal ceremonies as mentioned in this chapter. In this section, with the help of Tonita, she describes the ceremonies before entering the temazcal and the rituals inside of the sweat lodge.

Before entering Tonita's temazcal, Rita organized an outdoor circular altar with a number of objects and plants and she explains the significance of most of the elements such as:

1. **Water,** which is needed to survive and is part of our daily lives.

2. **Fire** represents Father Sky, who gives our body warmth.

3. **Conch Shell** sound represents the wind and the spiral form of the shell is the continuance of the work that is done from the beginning to the end.

4.  **Rattle and Drum** helps us reflect, and the sound of the drum signifies the beat of our heart and representing water.

5.  **Whistles,** made of clay animal figurines, emit a sound representing animals, birds, and water.

6.  **Flowers** are essential offerings taken from Mother Nature.

7.  **Copal incense** represents the smoke that will take our thoughts and intentions to the heavens. This incense is also used in the ceremony to honor the four directions.

8.  **Obsidian stone** comes from Mother Earth and represents our own reflection.

Rita commented that the above elements would be used during the opening ceremony to the four directions (east, west, north, and south) the heavens, the earth and our hearts. She offered some general comments on what to expect when we first experience the temazcal, such as entering the womb of Mother Earth and enjoying a sacred corner where we could sing, reflect, harmonize, and liberate emotions and toxins. She reminded us that we would experience a mixture of feelings, and transformation of thoughts and emotions.

After her comments, she asked the group of about 10 participants to take an instrument that was in the circular altar, such as a drum, rattle, or clay whistle, and use it during the ceremony to the four directions. Rita took the copal incense and asked the group to take an instrument from the altar, to stand in a circle, and to raise their open hands to the direction of the east. Holding the incense burner with copal smoke visible, she said, "I ask permission of the direction of the east, where the sun rises and helps our consciousness of a new day, and I ask it to strengthen our spirit. I offer this smoke of copal, the sound of the conch shell, and all of the instruments." As Rita raised her incense burner in a circular motion, Tonita blew on the conch shell horn (also called shell trumpet), I produced drum sounds, and the others used rattles and whistles for a cacophonous sound. Rita asked us to turn left facing the direction of the west, and she stated, "I ask permission of the direction of the west, a place of darkness and reflection in the night. A place where women who have passed on during childbirth rest and we ask for strength and tranquility."

The ritual of copal smoke and the sound of the various instruments were repeated for all of the other direction. The third direction was toward the north and Rita thanked our grandparents and ancestors for sharing their medicine and traditions. The fourth direction was to the south, a place of laughter, children, mountains, rivers, birds, and flowers and she asked for strength in continuing uniting the medicine and respecting Mother Nature. She requested that the group make a complete turn, facing each other and to raise their open hands to the heavens and the sacred sky, asking permission to continue sharing this medicine. After another complete circle to the left she asked us to honor Mother Earth by going to our knees and thanking the earth for giving us our daily bread. The final direction was taking our hands to our heart and singing a song, while Rita smudged everyone in the circle with copal smoke and afterwards scattered fresh rose petals on the heads of each person as if doing a blessing.

Before ending the ceremony, Rita welcomed and blessed a newly born baby being held by her mother by smudging her with copal incense and placing white rose petals on her small body symbolizing purity and repeating, "We honor your life, your mother and father and thank Mother Nature for allowing you to feel the light and love, and that you always have sacredness, hopefulness, and tenderness." Finally, Rita, asked the mother to place the baby next to her heart and she blew the conch shell horn around the child and mother, allowing the sound to encircle them for a final blessing before entering the temazcal and welcoming the infant into the tradition.

## Entering the Temazcal

Before entering the temazcal, Tonita offers her interpretation of the symbolisms of the sacred sweat lodge by reminding the group that the temazcal's oval structure represents the womb of Mother Earth and a place where we can leave unwanted emotions and where we will be reborn. She continues, "Once you enter the temazcal, look up at the dome and you will see a small hole that lets in a light beam representing the belly button of Mother Earth." This hole in the ceiling is about two inches and is useful in airing the temazcal, providing a bit of light, lowering the temperature, and clearing any smoke. Tonita continues, "As you enter, you will see the *texintle/tezontle*, or rocks, representing the ovaries of Mother Earth and the fire to heat the rocks represents the sperm. She reminds the group, "Together, you have the dual energies for healing and you will enter into the darkness to be reborn and cleanse, not only our body's lymphatic system, but also your spirit and soul." As each member of the group entered the small opening of the temazcal, they were given a plastic bucket of water and a washcloth to rub the body, in order to exfoliate and remove dead cells and rinse the cloth in the bucket of water. The individuals were each given a bundle of fresh **Basil** or ***Albahaca*** plant used for calming and relaxing. As each person entered the temazcal, they would get on their knees and utter the word *Ometeotl* (pronounced *O me teo*) a Nahuatl word meaning a dual cosmic energy. According to Tonita it means, "I see the divine in you and me, the good and bad, and the male and female in each person." They all entered from left to right and sat on a bench surrounding the temazcal, or they could sit on the floor, which was covered with aromatic plants.

### Inside the Temazcal

Once everyone was inside the warm temazcal, including the mother and child, Rita welcomed the group and asked permission of the hot volcanic rocks calling them *abuelitas*, grandmothers, calling the *abuelito*, grandfather fire and the plants for giving us life. She took the large drum in the center of the lodge and began chanting, *"he ya, he ya, he ya, he ya"* while the others joined the melody while producing other sounds with the rattles. Rita asked the group to yell out at the same time any petitions or needs they had.

She took a bundle of Basil plants, stood, and began fanning the area in order to reduce the temperature of the temazcal. She then asked the group to stand and to take their bundle of Basil herbs and to hit their body with the plants from head to toe, yelling at the same time *"ha ha ha."* This exercise was meant to stimulate our body's endorphins and toxins, as well as release fear, anger, insecurity, and pain. Everyone joined Rita in a second song to honor the drum, *"tamborcito tamborcito, ayudame a sanar"/* "little drum, little drum, help me heal."

After the song, Rita asked the mother to lie on the temazcal floor and took the baby. While rocking the baby back and forth, she sang a native lullaby. Rita and the mom stood up and Rita, still holding the infant, offered her words of wisdom and reminded the mother to leave her fears in the temazcal. She returned the baby to the mother.

After about an hour in the temazcal everyone left the lodge, bowed at the door, and crawling backward repeating the word *Ometeotl* as they departed. Once outside, the group gathered in a circle for a toast, raising a glass of herbal tea for a final blessing by Rita.

**Conclusion:** After a 20-year experience with a number of sweat lodges, beginning with the Lakota tradition and now with the Mexican temazcals, I can understand the concept of rebirthing, since after the steam bath, in combination with the ceremonies, I feel renewed and energized, realizing that I have received a rebirthing and a holistic cleansing of body, mind, and spirit. It is a revival of a spiritual feeling similar to what one has after a church service, repenting of sins and receiving the body of Christ through communion. With the recent revival of temazcals throughout Mexico and in some parts of the Southwest, I can see that our society will be healthier with this experience. I just hope that this tradition is not exploited by some who are untrained and using it for profits and selfish reasons.

**Figure 8.2** As part of the ritual inside of a temazcal, the aroma of the plants and the vibrations of the drums provide a powerful therapy for many.

# CHAPTER 9
# Healing with Laughter, Sound, and Music

You have met Chenchito in the first chapter, "Chenchito, the last of the Fidencista Healers," my teacher and mentor of traditional medicine for more than 20 years ago. I was fascinated to observe Chenchito with groups of followers of the Fidencista traditional healing movement, especially when he invited musicians to sing and play lively songs such as *corridos* (Mexican popular ballads) while encouraging everyone in the group to sing along, dance, and laugh. I overheard a comment Chenchito made to a sick lady that would not dance by saying, "Come, you're not as sick as you think you are, it's all in your head. Let's dance." Before his death, at the age of 90 Chenchito visited the University of New Mexico in Albuquerque. During his vist at a ceremonial event, he began, without music, clapping his hands and singing to a group of students, asking them to dance, and they did. Chenchito's singing, dancing, and laughing, especially with sick individuals, were similar to what the famous healer of the 1920s, Niño Fidencio, did with many of his patients. This is part of the *Fidencista* movement (healings and followers of the healer Fidencio). In many ways, the late Niño Fidencio and Chenchito were ahead of their time and believed that music and laughter were part of the healing process, without any research or clinical studies.

Nowadays, we read about Norman Cousins and how he healed himself of a life-threatening illness by watching funny films and constantly laughing, or Dr. Lee Berk whose studies indicate that laughter releases the stress hormones such as cortisol and produces dopamine that calms you and reduces anxiety. Moreover, there is Dr. Hunter Doherty "Patch" Adams, who dresses as a clown and brings humor to his patients, especially children, allowing the healing to accelerate. I do not believe the healer, Niño Fidencio, my mentor, Chenchito, or my colleague and curandera, Rita Navarrete, knew any of these people when they incorporated Laugh Therapy into their healing practices. In the following chapter on Laugh Therapy, Rita will do a brief demonstration of how she performs a laughter exercise with a group.

Juan Carlos Solano Alcocer *Xihuacatl* (his Aztec name) and his partner Viridiana, known as Viri, will discuss and demonstrate healing with the conch shell horn sound, in combination with the power of the sacred obsidian stone. Like many of the healers in this book, Juan Carlos has revived a lost tradition that was used by the native tribes of Mexico, specially the Aztecs, for hundreds of years.

In the last subchapter, a professional interpreter will share a few important points. Elena Klaver is from the state of Colorado, has been a part of the summer class on curanderismo for several years, and is multi-talented. She is an Aztec dancer, *danzante,* an excellent musician, and a recognized spiritual healer. Elena offers an excellent presentation on healing with the vibrations of music and sound. Elena will explain the sounds of a number of traditional rattles, whistles, and the drum, and how they may assist in traditional healing.

## 9.1 LAUGH THERAPY *(RISATERAPIA)*

A few years ago I attended a continuing education class on laughter, conducted by Clinical Psychologist, James Masica. Some of James' concepts of laughter included the reduction of negativity and hostility, and increasing efficiency and morale. He also discussed Norman Cousins' book, *Anatomy of an Illness* (Cousins, 2005) that recognizes the benefits of laughter such as lowering blood pressure and strengthening the immune system. After this enjoyable workshop, I began reading on laughter's healing benefits and discovered that laughter boosts the immune system and reduces stress, which helps the body's resistance to bacteria and viruses. I read how the late Norman Cousins was diagnosed with a life-threatening disease, *ankylosing spondylitis*, and how viewing comic films for ten minutes would provide him with two hours of pain free sleep and may have helped in his recovery. I discovered how professor Dr. Lee Berk (1989) researched the positive benefits of laughter on the brain and body, how it reduces the stress hormone cortisol, and increases the neurochemical dopamine, to reduce anxiety.

What I learned from my teachers and healers, Chenchito and Rita, who have not done clinical research, is that laughter helps in the healing process and with the cause of many ailments such as stress and anxiety. In her Laugh Therapy demonstration with a group of five individuals, including myself, Rita begins the session by stating, "This is a noble and enjoyable therapy that relaxes our muscles and gets the same results as exercising for forty minutes." She begins a group exercise by asking everyone to relax and warm the body by moving and shaking their legs, arms, hips, and shoulders. In order to warm the throat, she asks the group to repeat the sound of *ah, ah, ah*. She comments to the group that if they have a pain or an emotion that is bothering them, they should visualize it, inhale deeply and exhale the emotion or pain with a loud sound of *ha, ha, ha*. She reminds the group to relax the body and keep repeating the *ha, ha, ha* song three or four times, each time increasing the volume and force of the sound. Since we accumulate lots of stress in the face, she added another exercise of stretching the mouth by opening it as wide as possible.

To address an exercise to release anger, she asked the group to form a fist, quickly throwing it backward a few times while loudly yelling the sound of *ho, ho, ho* and doing this for about a minute. Afterward, she asks to relax the body with a gentle and soft sound of *ah, ah, ah*. She asked the group to place their hands on their waist and quickly giggle the sound of *he, he, he*, while thrusting their hips forward. The next exercise was to do a range of laughing sounds such as *ha, ha, ha* to *he, he, he*, to *hi, hi, hi*. Rita completed the Laugh Therapy exercise by asking the group to hold hands, moving their arms, at the same time, up in the air, and thrusting them down, while laughing.

Finally, Rita asked the individuals how they felt. The comments made by the group were, "I feel looser, I have lots of oxygen and breath better, and I'm calm and awaken." Tonita commented that about eight years ago, a similar Laugh Therapy exercise had transformed her life and I can attest to this life-changing experience since I was in the audience when this happened to her.

**Conclusion:** I have seen Rita conduct Laugh Therapy a number of times, and each session is adapted to the audience and never the same. One of the most impressive Laugh Therapy demonstrations that Rita did was in Washington, D.C. when I joined her and Tonita to participate in a two-week International Folklife Festival, sponsored by the Smithsonian Center. The theme was Folklife and Cultural Heritage and it was held in a large tent, at the United States National Mall. This two-week event attracts more than a million people from around the country and different parts of the world. In her Laugh Therapy

Figure 9.1 Through Laugh Therapy, *risa terapia*, an individual can relieve stress and pain.

presentation, Rita was able to work with a couple hundred participants and had them moving and laughing for several minutes. Her talent and ability to touch and improve the lives of others through laughter has always amazed me.

## 9.2  HEALING THROUGH SOUND

Juan Carlos is recognized internationally for his healing modalities using the conch shell horn in combination with the obsidian stone. He has connected this tradition to the *Meshika* (also spelled *Mexica*) cosmovision. He has been director of community health organizations in several Mexican communities including those in the Yucatan Peninsula and is currently the director of a clinic of traditional medicine that includes a temazcal sweat lodge and is a member of the *Kalpulli Ome*. He is assisted in his presentation by his partner Viri, who is also a healer.

Juan Carlos will be discussing and demonstrating another ancient energetic limpia called *tonalli,* using the sound of the conch shell in combination with the sacred obsidian stone. He discusses a connection in his healing to the four directions (east, west, north, and south) that have been described in earlier chapters and how the conch shell and the obsidian stone are connected to two of these direction. The conch shell (referred to as *atecocolli* in the Nahuatl language) represents the direction of the east, a direction of light and wisdom. Its guardian is *Quetzalcoatl* and this Aztec deity of Meshika mythology is also called the Feathered Serpent. It is one of the most famous Aztec deities and according to Juan Carlos: "He is the representation of the transformation of humankind and the expansion of spirit through the wisdom we acquire, and through the sound of the conch shell horn. *Quetzalcoatl* speaks so that light, clarity and wisdom are introduced into the body of the patient."

He continues by informing us that the black obsidian stone represents the direction of the north, helps us observe our true selves, to realize the emotions that are harming us, and what we need to do to work on them, in order to heal ourselves. Its guardian is another Aztec deity, *Tezcatlipoca,* whose name means "Smoking Mirror." He is the patron of the night and the north and is the opposite of his brother, *Quetzalcoatl.* He teaches that we are our own enemy and responsible for our own actions. The black shiny obsidian is like a smoking mirror where we can see and reflect on ourselves. It is a representation of the force of *Tezcatlipoca,* and a connection to our ancestors.

Juan Carlos connects his limpia healing to the duality concept, *ometeotl,* which was referred to in the temazcal chapter. Before beginning the demonstration, Juan Carlos offers a prayer and asks permission of his patient who is lying on a mat, Juan Pablo, and of his guardians, spirits, and guides. The permission is to receive the energy in order to heal the body, heart, and soul of the patient. The navel of Juan Pablo is exposed, since this area is the most powerful energetic center where energy is received and released, and he is reminded to breathe slowly and deeply. He is asked to call in his guardians, protectors, and ancestors to participate in the healing.

The black, shiny mirror-like oval obsidian stone is carefully and ceremonially placed by Juan Carlos over Juan Pablo's navel, while a large conch shell horn is tapped on top of the stone three times. Juan Carlos blows the conch shell horn in one long continuous strong note over the patient's body, starting at the head and moving down to the feet. A second note is repeated beginning at

**Figure 9.2** Juan Carlos performs a traditional healing technique by using the vibrations of the conch shell, *atecocolli.*

the feet and moving to the head and around the body. The belief is that in this limpia, the sound of the sea shell horn is entering the body's cellular system and filling it with light and consciousness. The obsidian stone remains on Juan Pablo's naval area giving strength to his consciousness and connecting him to the direction of the north and his ancestors. Juan Carlos' assistant, Viri, performs an energetic scanning moving her open hands over the patient's entire body. Juan Carlos reminds him to continue deep breathing, and that with each breath he will feel more at peace and harmony.

Finally, the patient is told to bid farewell to his guardians, protectors, and ancestors and to thank them for their presence and messages. As the obsidian mirror is removed, the patient is asked to inhale. As he exhales he releases all the emotions of fear, anger, and sadness.

Viri explains the concepts of this limpia, such as the body being divided from the navel area down and from the naval area up, and that we have two arms, eyes, legs, and nostrils that represent our duality. She says that this limpia attempts to balance this duality of positive and negative energies.

The patient, Juan Pablo, was asked if he felt dizzy and if so, this feeling was normal, since his energy had expanded and his body was adapting to this new energy. Juan Carlos commented, "Many people experiencing this type of limpia and feel as though they have grown, but it isn't that they have grown just that their energy has expanded."

**Conclusion**: It is apparent that Juan Carlos has researched the Mesoamerican cosmovision as it relates to the influences of *Quetzalcoatl* and *Tezcatlipoca,* and an ancient energetic limpia using the conch shell horn and the sacred black obsidian stone. His limpia cleansing is unique since the vibrations of the conch shell appear to impact the body's cellular system. In combination with the obsidian crystal stone, this has a positive impact on the patient. With some studies and research, his innovative and creative healing methods may prove to be confirmed as advanced medicines.

## 9.3 HEALING WITH MUSIC

Elena Klaver has many talents such as being a professional interpreter who travels around the world to interpret, mostly from Spanish to English. She is also a talented musician and composer of original songs, she is a *danzante* (dancer of traditional Aztec dance), and a traditional healer. She has been assisting my annual two-week class on curanderismo for several years as an interpreter, and presenter, and has taped a video for an online class module lesson on **Healing with Music**.

As a child, I remember waking up to the lively radio music with the sounds of Mexican polkas and *corridos* (ballads) that were popular during those years. There were times that dad and mom would dance with my four sisters, my brother, and me. In the evenings, we would have neighborhood sing-alongs and dances in a number of homes. The music, sing-alongs, and dances offered a positive attitude especially at the beginning of the day, allowed us to socialize within the families in our neighborhood, and kept us healthy with sound vibrations that impacted our cellular makeup.

Elena begins her presentation by recognizing and thanking a number of colleagues and musicians that have made an impact in her musical career and shares some quotes such as, " Music is the soul of the people/*musica es el alma del pueblo*," and "Music soothes the savage beast," referring to our feelings. Another descriptive quote concerning music is attributed by some to Plato, "Music gives a soul to the universe, wings to the mind, flight to the imagination and life to everything."

During my visits to the Cancer Center at the University of New Mexico's Health Sciences Center, I am always impressed with the live music that calms, soothes, and reduces stress with many patients. In Dr. Michael Friedman's article, "Does Music Have Healing Powers" in *Psychology Today*, he comments, "First of all, music has positive effects. It can produce direct biological changes such as reducing heart rate, blood pressure, and cortisol levels" (2014).

Elena discusses the impact of music, sound, and song on our health and refers to them as vibrations. She connects these sounds from the knowledge of indigenous traditions that invoke energies and vibrations, to that of quantum physics, that addresses the behavior of energy and matter. She emphasizes that everything is vibration and can be helpful, such as the soothing sound of running water and listening to beautiful music, or it can be destructive, such as a military ship's vibrations that harm whales and dolphins.

**Figure 9.3** Elena demonstrates how the drum can resemble the heartbeats of Mother Earth and our own.

As part of the healing practices, most cultures use a number of vibrations through healing songs, mantras, sounds, and spiritual chants, or through a variety of instruments used for invocations, such as the following, described and demonstrated by Elena:

1. **Drum:** Drumming is an ancient method of promoting healing and is practiced in a number of cultures throughout the world. In New Mexico, it is the custom of several Native American tribes to use drumming for a number of ceremonies, rituals, and celebrations. In my summer class, I offer a session, "The Medicine of the Drum," where our presenters discuss the health benefits of drumming, such as the reduction of stress and anxiety. Elena discusses the drum sound being the heart of Mother Earth, since its sound approximates our own heart beat. She drums and sings a beautiful native medicine song that allows the patient to be harmonious and in tune with himself/herself and others.

2. **Rattles:** Elena shares a number of rattles from different cultures, especially the *ayoyotes* (also called Aztec Jingles) that are hard shells derived from the *ayoyote* tree, *Thevetia genus*, and tied to the ankles and wrists of *danzantes*. They make the idiophone vibration sound of rain which is used in the ceremony of the four directions. Elena uses a rattle and sings a bilingual Nahuatl and Spanish song in order to keep the energy moving.

3. **Flutes:** Elena shows a number of clay figurine flutes that are used in ceremonies and healings. She demonstrates the sound of air and wind, a flute producing a number of tones. If our eyes are closed, the sounds can transport us to a different place and setting, as if we are eagles flying over the Andean Mountains. Elena's favorite clay flute resembles a large bird that produces a soothing and relaxing sound that she uses in performing limpias.

4. **Voice Sound:** Elena shares a group ritual that is also used in treating susto. The person suffering a susto experience is placed in the middle of a group of friends, and the group begins chanting her or his name in a harmonious, soft, and loving manner. The vibration sounds of the name can be very therapeutic. Elena quotes Jonathan Goldman: "Sound plus intention equals healing."

5. **Song:** Music can have an impact on human feelings such as we see in the importance of the Civil Rights Movement song, "We Shall Overcome." Songs can be powerful influences on social movements and are used in the temazcal as part of healing rituals. Elena sings one of her original songs based on an internationally popular number by Chilean composer, Violeta Parra, "*Gracias a la Vida*"/"Thanks to Life". Elena's song is entitled, "*Gracias a la Tierra Que Me ha Dado la Vida*"/"Thanks to the Earth Which has Given me Life." In her song, Elena thanks Father Sky for the sun, moon and clouds and Mother Earth for the air, wind, rain, and corn. This is an appropriate song that allows us to reflect on and appreciate what Mother Nature gives us, including her medicine.

**Conclusion**: Elena Klaver has shared with us her musical talents and interpretations of the healing power of music, including the vibrations of sounds through a number of instruments, and the power of song. She is creative in addressing susto by gathering a group of friends who repeat, in harmony, the name of the person suffering from what could be classified as Post-Traumatic Stress Syndrome (PTSD). In traditional medicine, I am always impressed with the simple methods of dealing with major health problems.

# PART 2
# GLOBAL PERSPECTIVES

# CHAPTER 10

# Introduction to the Influences of African Folk Healing

During a trip to Seville, Spain, I was fascinated with the arches, domes, and sunken gardens built as a royal palace for Moorish Muslim kings and La Giralda, a renaissance type cathedral with a North African Islamic minaret for its bell tower. Both structures are reminders of the armies of the Moors whose conquest of Spain began in 711 AD and lasted more than 800 years. I have yet to visit the famous Alhambra in Granada, Spain, an impressive fortress built by the rulers Yusuf I and Mohammed V. The invasion of Spain by the Moors influenced their culture in areas such as astronomy, mathematics, philosophy, music, and traditional medicine.

The Spaniards arrival to the New World, to what is now Mexico, in 1519, was the beginning of explorers bringing influences from Moorish-North African traditional medicine, such as herbal medications and rituals similar to the ones described in this book. Some of the African-Moorish rituals were changed with the introduction of Christianity, especially the form of the prayers and beliefs about God. It is important to be aware of the fact that both through the Mid-Atlantic slave trade and through the North African presence in Spain, Africa has influenced curanderismo.

I recently learned that a Registered Nurse from Albuquerque, Vodra Dorn, has been researching the traditional holistic medicine of African slaves brought to the United States. A nurse since the late 1970s, Mrs. Dorn knows both traditional and modern medicine and believes that both can complement one another. Her research has uncovered many of the herbal treatments of the African slaves such as a spring tonic made of garlic, rum to prevent illnesses and energize the children, and dried watermelon seeds for kidney stones. Two remedies that she discussed and that I also remember as a child, are small pouches of *asefetida* worn around the neck to prevent illnesses and diseases. The pouch contained a number of strong herbs such as ginseng, pokeweed, and yellow root. A second remedy that is now prohibited was paregoric for babies with colic, which contained camphor, aniseed, and benzoic acid. Mrs. Dorn states, "We all have the healing abilities within our hands and need to move away from popping a pill for every ache and pain. And going back to nature for healing is something that Americans need to get back to."

During a visit to my summer curanderismo class by a group of Ugandan traditional healers and an allopathic physician that incorporates traditional medicine in his practice, I learned that African traditional medicine continues using herbal medicine and spiritualism similar to some of the practices in Mexico, Central, and South America. The frequent usage of African traditional medicine is comparable to many other developing countries because of its low cost, the lack of health clinics in rural areas, and a lengthy cultural tradition dating back hundreds of years. These are all factors that contribute to its popularity.

During the visit by the healer from Uganda, I learned that the usage of herbal medications, the offering of incense for energetic/spiritual cleansings, and several healing rituals, were similar to ones used by Mexican curanderos(as) and described in this book. Bokaye Ndong Mba from Gabon, Africa, a small country off the

Atlantic coast of Central Africa, was another healer who shared his healing music techniques using a rustic harp and chants similar to the ones in the earlier chapters, addressing healing through sound and music, introduced by Juan Carlos and Elena.

## 10.1 AFRICAN TRADITIONAL MEDICINE FROM UGANDA

I met Sarah Nsigaye at the University of New Mexico campus about six months before my summer class on traditional medicine. Sarah stopped by my office and introduced herself as the Executive Director of Native Travel Festival. She told me about her nonprofit organization established in 2010 that serves two million Ugandans in sixty villages with an annual **Celebration of Womanhood Festival** and an **Indigenous Knowledge Expo**. Sarah was in New Mexico visiting friends, heard about my class on curanderismo, and was interested in bringing a number of traditional healers from Uganda to the class so they could share their traditional medicine that was practiced by about 80% of the villagers, but shunned by the medical establishment.

After a lengthy conversation about our collaborations with Mexican healers on herbology and traditional healing techniques, Sarah and I realized that we shared a number of similarities in traditional medicine practices, and I decided to welcome the Ugandan visitors as my guests to the summer class. In mid-July they attended most of the two-week class on traditional medicine with lectures from a number of local healers from the Southwest and Mexico. The Ugandan visitors also presented to the class a number of sessions such as:

1. **Promoting Ugandan Traditional Medical Knowledge:** This presentation was given by Dr. Sekagya Yahaya, a physician and director of PROMETRA, a forest school for traditional health practitioners founded as a result of poor health conditions in Uganda and a lack of modern health services. Dr. Sekagya discussed the mission of the program: "harnessing nature and promoting good health, with the vision of a healthy, well informed and productive population." The PROMETRA nonprofit organization developed a large medicinal garden, a second garden of nutritional food plants, a health clinic, a dormitory, an outdoor kitchen and dining hall, a traditional medicine processing plant, and a number of indoor and outdoor classes.

2. **Packaging, Processing, and Marketing Herbal Medicine:** Daudah Mayanja discussed an herbal plant venture started by his late father for processing, packaging, and marketing a number of medicinal plants for the general public of Uganda. He stressed quality control and proper cultivation of the medicinal plants for public consumption. He displayed a number of popular plants that are being offered to the general population of Uganda and neighboring African countries at nominal prices.

3. **How Traditional Birth Attendant Practice Has Evolved:** Sarah Nsigaye shared with us the history of midwifery in Uganda and Africa, and how the knowledge of midwives was traditionally passed down from mother to daughter, or other close family members. Recently, the practice of midwifery has changed with the collaboration of health professionals that train women on pregnancy, childbirth, treating the postpartum period, and the care of the newborn. Other services provided by the midwife are education about women's health and reproductive health.

4. **Combating Cancer with Native Medicine:** Dr. Victor Kiwalabye is the Senior Herbal Consultant with Victor Herbalist Research Association in Kampala, Uganda. Dr, Kiwalabye discussed the role he has assumed for the last 20 years in the fight against cancer and HIV/AIDS infections, and nutritional deficiencies, using traditional herbal medicine.

During their visit, a reception was hosted by the university's Maxwell Museum of Anthropology to honor the Ugandan healers with a special performance by Bokay Ndong Mba from Gabon, on healing with music.

The Ugandan healers were invited to do a video at the University of New Mexico for an online course on the "**Global Influences of Curanderismo.**" The following is a summary of their comments in addition to my personal input and interpretations:

Sarah, the group's leader, introduced the healers and stated that some of them were considered spiritualist healers who held the belief that illness is not necessarily caused by a bacteria or virus but through a spiritual or social imbalance. Others were traditional healers with the knowledge of herbal medicine, with its preparation of teas, ointments, and tinctures. One of the healers, Dr. Sekagya Yahaya, used both methods of healing (spiritual and traditional) with the incorporation of allopathic modern medicine, since he was a physician trained as a dental surgeon.

Sarah mentioned that indigenous and traditional medicine in Africa, and in the country of Uganda, is at risk, since modern medicine has a tendency to marginalize it, especially in the rural communities where 90% of the people use traditional medicine. Her goal was that traditional medicine complement modern allopathic medicine, as is the case in China, some parts of the United States, and other countries. Promoters of traditional medicine believe that it should be integrated into allopathic modern medicine, instead being a complementary or an alternative medicine.

Dr. Sekagya, is a physician who has maintained his African roots and has incorporated traditional and spiritual medicine into his practice. He explained that African traditional medicine uses a holistic approach to healing physical, spiritual, moral, and social elements and when these function are in balance, a person is healthy. However, when one of these features is not in balance, a person becomes ill, physically, emotionally, or spiritually. Dr. Sekagya used an example, "If a person is slapped, they might cry, not because of the physical pain, but because of the embarrassment and a physical substance, in the form of medicine, cannot take that away. But, if we use smoke to call the ancestors, they might intervene in the operation and that might resolve the emotional trauma." He mentioned that this spiritual issue, if not treated, could manifest as a physical ailment. Dr. Sekagya was discussing a limpia using smoke or incense to help with the trauma (what curandero/as call susto). He demonstrated a number of incense samples that he called essence and he stated that they were used for a number of needs such as expressing gratitude, relationship problems, and for good luck and prosperity.

The Ugandan group live in an area that grows coffee plants and they used the coffee beans for a healing therapy. While the coffee beans remain in their shells, they are shared with a group of friends and family members. After removing the beans from their shells, each person chews the beans, therefore bringing the group together in a ceremony for the sharing of a communal food and forming one united body. This practiced reminded me of receiving the body of Christ in communion during a Christian church service. In addition to eating coffee beans, a ceramic incense burner, like the Mexican *sahumerio*, is used and the incensed burned is similar to Mexican *copal*. It produces a pleasant smelling smoke that cleanses the group and takes the energies to the heavens. It is believed that the spirits of their ancestors, departed love ones, and those of friends, join the group during this period.. The ceremony is completed with an African chant and lively body movements. This ceremony resembles Laurencio's limpias or Rita's temazcal ceremonies.

Daudah Mayanja is an herbalist that learned to identify medicinal plants from his late father. He developed a business in Uganda and other African countries that promotes and markets traditional

**Figure 10.1** Ugandan group of traditional healers and Dr. Eliseo Torres discuss the African traditional herbal remedies.

medications with proper research, packaging, and quality control. He discussed the bartering concept, which is based upon exchanging animals such as chickens and cows for his medications, a concept that has been lost in this country but continues to thrive in Africa. Mr. Mayanja is providing a service to the majority of the African population that live in rural areas and may not have access to many of the medicinal herbs that come from different regions and rain forests.

**Conclusion:** In comparing the traditional medicine of Africa to that of Mexico, there are many similarities especially in treating the person's mind, body, and spirit; however, the African traditional medicine practice has added the moral and social functions making this a holistic approach to healing that goes beyond the physical body. A parallel form of limpia was evident in the usage of essence or incense, coffee beans, honoring ancestors, and chanting, similar to the Mesoamerican ceremony of honoring the four directions with copal incense, song, and recognition of the ancestors. The challenge with the Ugandans is the lack of recognition of their traditional medicine by the medical profession and a need for research with the plants and rituals.

## 10.2   AFRICAN HEALING THROUGH MUSIC FROM GABON

I met Angie Thompson when she was a student enrolled in the Honors Program at the University of New Mexico. She had just returned from a study abroad program in Gabon and met with me to discuss her experiences in this equatorial Francophone country on the west coast of Central Africa that was ruled by France until 1960. Angie was aware that I was teaching a university course on curanderismo and asked if I would invite, as a presenter to the class, a person she had met in Gabon by the name of Bokaye Ndong Mba. Bokaye was considered a spiritual healer called an *N'ganga*, an important member of his community. He performed healing rituals through the chants and music of the traditional *Ngombi* harp. He also incorporated other homemade elements into his healings like the *Mogongo* one-string musical instrument and the *Tika* horn. I agreed to invite Bokaye and also to have him join another group of healers from Uganda who were scheduled to join me during the summer course. Bokaye only spoke French and his native Fang language, but that was not a problem since Angie was fluent in French.

In addition to an excellent presentation to the class on the Bwiti religion and its spiritual and healing rituals, Bokaye taped a video presentation for our traditional medicine program, and Angie would join us as an interpreter from French to English. In this chapter, I have attempted to summarize his presentation and have added my comments based on the similarities and comparisons to Mexican traditional healing.

In his presentation, Bokaye described the Bwiti religion of the forest people of Gabon and how it views the world around them such as seeing the soul of plants and belief in ancestor veneration. He mentioned the connection with the root bark of the *Tabernanthe Iboga* plant, which is used for religious rituals. It induces visions and promotes spiritual growth, bringing family and community together, and helping resolve problems. After asking him to give me additional information on the Bwiti religion, I discovered that it is one of three recognized official religions in the country of Gabon. The following are the instruments, songs, and clay paint that Bokaye described as part of the rituals used in the Bwiti religion:

1.  *Mogongo* **Musical Instrument:** According to Bokaye, *Mogongo* was the first musical instrument that the Bwiti religion uses in order to allow man to communicate with the spirits through its sounds and vibrations. The *Mogongo* is a curved piece of wood resembling an arched bow with one stretched string attached to each end. The instrument is placed upright on the player's leg and against his chest, with the string next to his lips. By the tapping of the string with a stick, it produces different rhythms, tones, and vibrations. The wood has a natural arch bent and each *Mogongo* is unique. The interpretation of the sacred object is that the string represents the sky, the wooden arch represents the Earth, and that God sees everything that happens between the sky (string) and Earth (wooden arch).

Therefore, as human beings cannot see God, believers in the ceremony are not allowed to view the musician playing the the sacred *Mogongo* that also connects us with our ancestors. The tradition teaches that if women see the instrument before entering the ceremonial temple, the wood changes and distorts the sound. The vibrations of the *Mogongo* transform the person being initiated or healed at a spirit level, and allows their guardians and ancestors to be with them.

**Figure 10.2** Healer from Gabon, plays the Mogongo musical instrument, which is used in his tradition to communicate with the spirits.

1. ***Tika* Horn:** The Tika horn resembles the Jewish *Shofar* ram horn and is used to call the spirits to the ceremony. This particular animal horn has a white tip and a black body, which are two of the three official colors used in the Bwiti religion, with the third color being red. The horn is blown through a hole bored on the side and Bokaye plays it four times turning to the left while calling the energies of the planets in the four directions to join him. This resembles the ceremonies of the four directions (east, west, north,and south) that most of the curanderos(as) use in ceremonies and which is described throughout this book.

2. **Kaolin Clay Face Paint:** After the *Tika* horn is played, Bokaye applies a Kaolin (natural mineral clay) colored powdered to his face. White Kaolin clay is placed about an inch wide, above his eyebrows and across his forehead, representing the spirits of the forest and water. The color white is traditionally used only by men. The second color that he places vertically between his eyebrows is the color red, derived from the red bark of the Padauk tree. This color is used in order to connect the energies and represents blood. Red is reserved for women only. However, Bokaye uses both colors, white and red in order to show the connections with both sexes, similar to the Aztec *Ometeotl* concept of duality represented by man and woman in one person.

3. ***Ngombi* Harp:** The *Ngombi* is an eight-string harp instrument about two feet long in the shape of a wooden woman wearing a red crown with the strings connected to her torso. According to Bokaye, the figure of the woman represents love and the three colors of her dress are red, white, and blue, the official colors of the Bwiti religion. The belief is that the *Ngombi* harp is replacing the *Mogongo* sound, whose energy and spirits are now weak and departing. Bokaye completes his presentation of the ceremony by playing the *Ngombi* harp in a seated position and creating a number of tones by a fast strumming of the cords. Angie joins him by playing the rattles and dancing in rhythm in order to gain the attention of the spirits. Bokaye sings a song, while playing the harp, in honor of the Bwiti religion. He explains that every song has a significance, such as honoring the spirits, the ancestors, or love ones.

**Conclusion:** During the two-week summer curanderismo class at the University of New Mexico, I convened a session with Bokaye from Gabon, six healers from Uganda, ten curanderos(as) from Mexico, and about eight healers from New Mexico and other parts of the Southwest. They sat in a circle with a number of students joining them in an outer circle. The objective of this event was to discuss the differences and similarities between the forms of traditional healing in their cultures. To my surprise, there were many more similarities than differences. They all performed spiritual cleansings, they honored their ancestors and the four directions, they used medicinal plants, musical instruments, song, and dance. It was a consensus that they all had an obligation and devotion to serve their community, especially in physical, mental, and spiritual needs. Bokaye's presentation of the Bwiti religion, including healing rituals using musical instruments like *Mogongo*, *Tika* horn, and the *Ngombi* harp, reminded me of Elena Klaver's chapter on "Healing through Music," in which she emphasized the concept that vibrations impact our cellular system. These vibrations, songs, and chants are part of the holistic healing practices, and are integrated into the spiritually recognized religion of Bwiti, which is also similar to Chenchito's Fidencista movement mentioned in a previous chapter. Unlike Gabon's Bwite, Fidencismo has not been recognized as an official religion.

# CHAPTER 11
# Contributions of Afro-Latino Healing

## 11.1   INTRODUCTION TO AFRO-LATINO TRADITIONAL HEALING

African culture is evident in almost all Caribbean Islands, Central, and Latin American countries, especially in music, dance, art, and traditional medicine. In the next three subchapters, Sina-Aurelia Tuuau Sao discuss a spiritual limpia through drumming and dance honoring the four directions. The second subchapter describes the African influences in Cuba through a presentation and demonstration by a Cuban *Santero* healer from Havana, Pedro Palacios, who is assisted by a student of *Santeria*, David Hernandez. A third *Santero* who is originally from Puerto Rico but is currently a professor at a college in California, Dr. Ysamur Flores, shares a ritual using different colored fabric and plants.

All three presenters discuss a unique spiritual cleansing with roots in Africa but with some changes and modifications adapted to their environment and talents. Sina uses her professional training in song, dance, and music in her limpia, while Pedro uses the natural elements of Cuba, which include cigar smoke, plants, and a coconut. Ysamur also uses plants and different colors, and chants, for a Puerto Rican limpia. All three demonstrations have several elements in common with the spiritual cleansing performed by the healers from Uganda and Gabon, and Mexican curanderismo.

## 11.2   AFRO-LATINO HEALING THROUGH MUSIC AND DANCE

Sina-Aurelia Tuuau Sao's talents are similar to those of Elena Klaver who has contributed to the previous chapter on "Healing through Music." Sina is a socio-ethnomusicologist, a traditional healer, and a *griot*. The *griot* are West African singers, storytellers, and musicians.

Sina explains that her type of spiritual cleansing is an indigenous fusion including a sacred ceremony and honoring the four directions. She is joined by Mensa, a master drummer, who uses different drum sounds according to the phase of the ritual. In initiating the ceremony, Sina is attempting to unblock the heart chakra that brings joy and inner peace, and seeks to stimulate the third chakra in the upper abdomen that addresses self-confidence.

She begins her opening ceremony by performing a dance with particular steps, and turns in honor of the four directions (east, west, south, and north). She continues to recognize Father Sky by lifting her hands to the heavens and to the ground by

Figure 11.1 Sina demonstrating the ritual of honoring the Four Directions through dance and the vibrations of the drum.

thanking Mother Earth. She completes this phase of the ceremony by placing her hand to her chest to honor her heart. A chant is recited in order to awaken the senses and call the energies of the divinity to join her.

During a second and more powerful chant, she once again motions to the four directions and moves clockwise in order to open the sacred space and acknowledges the four elements, which will be used in the limpia ceremony, including fire, water, earth, and air. The following four elements, in addition to honoring the four directions, are the central theme of Sina's spiritual cleansing:

1. **Fire:** To acknowledge the fire element, Sina burns a bundle of white sage plant, called a sacred smudge stick, which is used by many Native Americans in purifying and blessing people and spaces. According to Sina, for *cólera*, which means extreme anger, she recommends a smudging with a dried lavender/*alucema* plant for a calming effect, to create balance and to placate the person's energy or spirits. For *tristeza,* or sadness, Sina recommends a smudging with dried *yerba buena*/spearmint. Sina smudges the person, using appropriate herb, while singing a soothing song, according the the mixolydian musical scale, and walking counter clockwise in order to remove the unwanted energy.

2. **Water:** After the smudging, Sina continues walking in a circle around the patient sprinkling water. The type of water can be *agua pura*/ pure water, holy water, sea water, or river water, depending on the type of treatment. Substitutes for water include tears or saliva.

3. **Earth:** Before the earth element is used during the closing ceremonies, a sacred wrap of *rafia* fibers (could also use grass, string, or yarn) is wrapped around Sina's right hand in order to open the energies. She would use her left hand to close them. Sina then binds the patient around the ribcage with a brightly colored belt, and with deepening drumming, she takes a handful of earth and walks around the person twice spreading the dirt and forming a circle. She has to choose how to bind the patient, depending on the need, around the ribcage, or the "third eye" (a mystical invisible perception that goes beyond sight, located on the forehead). The belief is that Sina is binding the negative energies that reside in the body and are responsible for the ailment. During her third walk, she takes a small amount of dirt and places it on the forehead and palms of the person's hands.

4. **Air:** It is through the air element that people are afflicted with mal de ojo/evil eye or *envidia*/envy, since it happens through negative vibrations passed through the air. The ceremony will allow these vibrations to be sent back to the direction they came from.

**Conclusion:** In addition to removing negative vibrations associated with the air element, the earth element is connected to physical touch and its negative energy will be returned to the earth. Anger and psychological, transgressive, negative energy is being burned with fire, while emotional trauma such as PTSD will be returned to water. In the final phase of the limpia, Sina takes the bundle of *rafia* fibers, or sacred grass related to the earth element and, with the beat of the drum, is swung and brushed over the patient, who is on the floor in a sitting position. The person is asked to stand and the sacred grass is passed throughout his or her body with sweeping motions, including over his legs and feet. During the ceremony, Sina is singing a healing song called *cante cura*, which activates the inner energies, and honors the ancestors and the four directions. She places her opened left hand against the lower back of the patient and her right hand will act as a conduit to send out the unwanted energy. She sings out the vowels "e ea a u" and asks the patient to repeat the sound while breathing through the nose and out through the mouth.

A final utterance acknowledged God as *Yahweh* with the sounds of the four syllables, *yod, hay, vav, hay*. These come from the Hebrew tradition that believes one should not directly use the name of God, which is too sacred to be spoken. Sina ties these four sounds to the four directions and refers to her energetic cleansing as an indigenous fusion since she is able to blend a number of African chants,

Native American white sage incense, rituals from curanderismo, and Hebrew religious beliefs. She does a comprehensive and holistic limpia in combination with song and dance.

## 11.3 AFRO-CUBAN HEALING TECHNIQUES

I met David Hernández while he was a librarian at Central New Mexico Community College, located next to the University of New Mexico. David and I discussed my work with Mexican curanderismo since he was also a healer and a follower of Cuban *Santeria*, a belief system with West African roots, especially from the *Yoruba* culture of southwestern Nigeria. It is also mixed with Christianity, other West and Central African traditions, and the indigenous traditions of the *Taino* people of the Caribbean. David suggested that I invite his *padrino* (godfather) Pedro Palacios from Havana, Cuba, who is a well-known *Babalawo* (*Ifa* healer/priest), *Santero*, and *Palo Monte* practitioner. He is recognized throughout Cuba as well as Florida and parts of the Southwest for his knowledge of medicinal plants of the Caribbean as well as for his expertise in a number of rituals. In July, Pedro joined us for a presentation to the students in the summer curanderismo class, as well as for a taping of a video for my semester online course. This chapter is a demonstration and discussion of two Cuban Santeros: Pedro and David. I have added my comments and opinions to the presentation of the santeros.

David clarified the *Santeria* ritual, interpreted the limpia performed by Pedro, and gave a brief history of *Santeria* with the Cuban term *Osha*, which he prefers, stating that it came from sources in Africa, mainly from the *Yoruba* and *Bantu* cultures during the 16th through 19th centuries. While David is talking, Pedro is drawing a circle on the floor using a chalk-like powder made with egg shells. David states that the circle represents a magical place for people to enter to receive healings, for ceremony, or just for a meditation. With the white chalk-like powder, Pedro divides the circle into four sections or quadrants. The Northwest direction of one quadrant represented the supernatural realm of spiritual powers and ancestors. Another showed four arrows representing the four winds and the air that surrounds us, as practiced in the *Palo Monte*, which comes from African slaves of Bantu-speaking origin. Another is representative of all the waters around us, including sea water and salt water. A skull is drawn in one quadrant while the moon, stars, and sun are seen in another one. There is an image that resembles an anchor in one section, and another with additional arrows. When Pedro completes the images on the circle, he sprays rum on the herbs as a final blessing. He draws arrows on the shins of his legs, forehead, and arms, with the white eggshells, and continues sprinkling the same powder on the herbs. He completes his blessing by lighting a cigar in order to smudge the altar, herbs, and circle.

The meaning of the arrows, David explains, is the circulation of energy in any magical action taken by the healer. Pedro and David describe the following three plants, typically used in a limpia from their tradition:

1. *Maravilla, Mirabilis multiflora,* **Four-O-Clock:** In addition to using this plant for a Cuban-style limpia, the black seeds are used topically for prostate problems. In parts of Mexico, it is used in liniments and ointments to relieve muscular aches associated with arthritis.

2. *Yerba Fina, Cynodon dactylon,* **Bermuda Grass:** There are many varieties of *Yerba Fina* and the most common is what we call Bermuda Grass. This is another plant used in Pedro's limpia, and it can also be pulverized and placed on open wounds to stop the bleeding.

3. *Vencedor. Vitex agnus-castus,* **Lilac Chaste Tree/Monk's Pepper:** *Vencedor* means winner, and in the spiritual world it is used for good luck and help with legal problems. This plant is prescribed medicinally to balance premenstrual and menstrual conditions. Before he steps into the circle, David reminds Bob Vetter (a cultural anthropologist who presents a section on Native American cleansing) that he is receiving the cleansing in order to connect with the waters, winds, stars, and spiritual realms. He is asked to remove his shoes and step into the circle that Pedro has created in order to

receive the limpia. Pedro begins by reciting a chant invoking the ancestors while sweeping Bob's body from head to toe with the bundle of *Yerb Fina*.

4. The second plant used for the cleansing is done with a different chant and with the bundle of the *Maravilla* herb, which is again used to sweep the body concentrated on the head, a seed of consciousness. The process is repeated with a third chant invoking Bob's spirits to protect him from harm and bring him success, while brushing his body with the *Vencedor* plant. Bob continues standing inside the circle and is asked to step on the three plants. In the next step of the limpia, Pedro uses a coconut to sweep Bob's body and,when finishing this ritual, places it inside the circle next to the plants.

**Figure 11.2** The smoke of the cigar and the coconut are important components to the spiritual cleansing, as demonstrated by Pedro on Bob.

David explains that the coconut is important in all Afro-Cuban rituals since this fruit is believed to be a communicator and mediator between the different planes of existence. A half-dried coconut shell dish is filled with rum, taken in Pedro's mouth, and sprayed throughout Bob's body (like the "breath of life") to strengthen his spirit. Pedro continues by lighting a Cuban cigar, turning it around with the hot coal inside his mouth and blowing smoke throughout Bob's body, similar to a smudging with Native American white sage or Mexican copal smoke. Finally, Bob is asked to do three small jumps insidethe circle and one larger one out of the circle, leaving all his negative energy inside the circle. The moment that Bob jumps out of the circle is important since everything that Pedro has been working on is left inside the magical circle or space.

**Conclusion:** Pedro and David remind us that all of the elements used in the spiritual cleansing were of nature, such as the three plants, the white powdered egg shell, the rum made with sugar cane, and the cigar made from a plant. Pedro is eclectic in his approach to *Santeria,* using different types of healing treatments and rituals and has been given titles such as *Tata, Babalola, Paleo, Malongo,* and *Curandero* describing the modalities and lineages he works in. This Afro-Cuban tradition showed us a comprehensive and holistic spiritual cleansing using elements similar to those used by Laurencio Nuñez from Oaxaca, Mexico, in his limpia, including the four elements of Mother Nature, wind, fire, water, and earth; however, in his limpia, Laurencio used Mezcal and copal, typical of his Oaxacan region; Pedro used rum as well as cigar tobacco, popular on the island of Cuba. They, as well as other healers described in this book, are able to adapt to what is available in their environment.

## 11.4 AFRO-PUERTO RICAN HEALING MODALITIES

Because of my class on *Curanderismo*, Dr. Ysamur M. Flores, who teaches at Otis College of Art and Design in California, joined me for the summer traditional medicine class. After meeting with Dr. Flores, I learned that he was born in Puerto Rico and received a BA from the University of Puerto Rico, his MA from the Pontifical University of Puerto Rico and PhD from the University of California in Los Angeles in Folklore and Mythology, which prepared him as a specialist in African-based religions in the New World. He has also published articles on *Santeria*. I was impressed that he came from three generations of priests (his mother, himself, and his son) in the *Lucumi* Afro-Caribbean traditions. Just as I had done with many of the talented and experienced visitors in my class, I invited him to do a video for the online course in order to learn from an expert in the Puerto Rican Afro-Caribbean healing traditions.

This chapter explains Dr. Flores' demonstration a type of *Osain* spiritual cleansing; *Osain* is considered the God of all healing plants. According to Dr. Flores, leaves of the *Vencedor* plant would be used in this *Osain* limpia, and he clarified that other spiritual cleansings could use flowers, smoke, and fire, similar to the elements discussed in earlier chapters. In addition to the leaves, fabric would be part of the limpia and would consist of two pieces of fabric of about two by two feet square. The following are the steps Dr. Flores took in performing his Osain spiritual cleansing:

**Figure 11.3** Dr. Ysamur Flores describes the use of black and red fabrics that will hold the energetic vibrations after the Osain spiritual cleansing.

1. **Red and Black Fibers:** One square of fabric was red, symbolizing life, while the second one was black, for death. The Western tradition uses white and black for the same purpose of life and death. Both fabrics were placed on the floor with the black square on top of the red, and the person receiving the limpia was asked to stand on the fabrics. The belief is that all negative energy is pulled from the person and transferred to the black fabric, while the red square with the positive vibration will wrap around the black one with life enveloping death.

2. **Vencedor Leaves:** The *Vencedor* plant is used in a number of Santeria rituals, as described in the previous chapter. The English common name is *Lilac Chaste Tree*, or *Monk's Pepper*. In spiritual terms, it is used to emit positive vibrations and absorb negative ones. Medicinally it is utilized to balance premenstrual and menstrual conditions. The person receiving the cleansing was asked by Dr. Flores to stand in front of the red and black fibers and he took the *Vencedor* plant and separated it into two bunches placing them on the person's head, a seed of intelligence and the soul. He began the limpia with a Lucumi traditional spiritual cleansing chant asking for the blessing of the creator, ancestors, spirits, and the energy of any priests to help with the *Sarayeye* cleansing ceremony. He took the bundles of plants in each hand and began sweeping the body from head to toe, periodically shaking the invisible negative energy from the plants on top of the black fabric. This was done while chanting an incantation in the *Lucumi* dialect.

3. **Closing the Limpia Ceremony:** After the incantation, Dr. Flores takes the *Vencedor* plant, breaks it up and placed the leaves on the black square. He takes two ends of the fabric and ties them together and repeats the process with the other ends. The four tied corners of the black fabric represented the four corners of the universe and were tied and secured so that no evil could come to the person or to the healer, Dr. Flores. The red fiber representing life and positive vibrations was wrapped around the black bundle and tied in the same fashion. The patient was asked to step over the bundle in the form of a cross representing the cross of the universe, rather than the Christian one. The patient now created a new crossroad of life, prosperity, beauty, and blessings. The bundle of the black and red fabric with the leaves would be disposed of in a different location.

**Conclusion:** By now, we can appreciate that types of energetic and spiritual cleansing techniques are unlimited and each tradition has its own style. The most important thing to remember in performing one is that there be a good and positive intention. Dr. Flores' family has three generations of practicing traditional medicine and spiritual healing, and he has done much research on the heritage of African-based religion and healings of *Santeria*. He is a true practitioner of this tradition. His writings, research, and practices indicated that, if done correctly, this type of healing can be beneficial in addressing one's spiritual, physical, and mental needs.

# CHAPTER 12

# Sacred Tobacco of Peru/Medicinal Plants for Women

In 2009, Asheninka Mino joined Bernadette Torres to initiate an outdoor school called "Shabeta's Healing Garden" that bridges Mino's Peruvian roots in traditional medicine with Bernadette's extensive experience, knowledge, and teaching of medicinal plants. Both have been regular lecturers in my two-week curanderismo summer class and were willing to make a video, as the other healers have done, in order to preserve their knowledge and wisdom. In this chapter, Bernadette discusses herbs for women, while Mino shares the usage of the sacred tobacco of Peru.

Mino was raised by his parents in the jungles of Peru learning the indigenous culture and was later mentored by a master visionary healer, *Kentzikuari,* who taught him the lessons of Mother Nature with the understanding of how to use medicinal plants. He is considered a healer, teacher, and ambassador for the indigenous *Asheninka* community of central jungle of Peru.

His partner, Bernadette Torres, is an herbalist, instructor, health facilitator, and the director of Shabeta's Healing Garden. She learned about medicinal plants from her father in the mountains of Taos, New Mexico, and conducts herb walks with students during the summer. She teaches at the nationally recognized New Mexico School of Natural Therapeutics. Bernadette agreed to do a demonstration on three herbs for women's sexual reproductive organs, also sharing with us about the medicinal usages of watermelon. Her presentation is followed by Mino's talk on the traditional medicinal and spiritual use of tobacco.

To initiate the talks by both healers, Mino did an opening blessing with sacred tobacco by smudging himself, Bernadette, me, and the space around us with the tobacco smoke coming from a traditional pipe.

After the blessing, Bernadette began her presentation by stating that her topic was herbs for the sexual reproductive organs, specifically because of their emotional significance. In addition to discussing the three medicinal herbs that she grew in her garden, she would also talk about the usage of the watermelon for a body cleansing. The plants and their medicinal usage were discussed as follows:

1. **English Marigold,** *Calendula/Pericon/Cempasuchil,* *Calendula officinalis***:** This is an anti-inflammatory plant with some antibacterial properties. Calendula oil is rubbed

**Figure 12.1** Asheninka Mino is performing an opening blessing on herbalist Bernadette Torres with sacred tobacco as done in Peru.

and massaged on the naval chakra to reduce inflammation and to bring a person into balance. Bernadette has used this technique and noticed that a number of emotions are released, so she asks the women to do a writing exercise in order to express what will bring them into balance. Calendula oil also balances the naval chakra, one that Eclectic Energies refers to as, "asserting yourself to the group. When it is open, you feel in control and you have sufficient self-esteem. When the naval chakra is under-active, you tend to be passive and indecisive. You're probably timid and don't get what you want. If this chakra is overactive, you are domineering and probably even aggressive." Bernadette states that men can also use the herb in the same manner.

2. **Dandelion, *Diente de Leon, Taraxacum officinale*:** The Dandelion plant is considered a weed that people pull up and throw away and one that we try to eradicate from our flower beds and gardens. According to Bernadette, it is a highly nutritious plant that is packed with vitamins and minerals. As a medicinal plant, Dandelion oil is used with women suffering from hard breast lumps, nodules, or nymphs that could lead to cancer. The oil is a lymph cleanser and can be used to massage the heart chakra. This herb can be used by men who can also develop breast cancer.

3. **Mullein, Gordolobo, Verbascum thapsus:** The Mullein plant is used to tonify the lungs. Bernadette makes a Mullein oil from the flowers in order to clear the throat area. She suggests using the oil in reproductive areas where women frequently have issues with their thyroid, when their hormones are getting out of balance. It is used with women experiencing menopause, which causes rashes and pain. She recommends the oil be massaged around the ears and into the jaws to help balance the throat chakra, especially for those women who tend to be quiet. Bernadette summarizes that when the naval, heart, and throat chakras are connected, it impacts the reproductive system and improves communication and expression.

4. **Watermelon:** Bernadette recommends a watermelon drink pureed in a blender and consumed for seven days as an excellent way to cleanse the body. Watermelon is nutritious and provides vitamins, minerals, and only a few calories. It addresses the root chakra located in the tailbone area, which is said by many people to be connected to issues of survival and incarnation.

5. For extreme cases, Bernadette will refer her clients to Mino who does his healing with sacred tobacco in order to balance the mind, body, and spirit. We know that excessive use of tobacco causes cancer and that even secondhand smoke also increases the risk of cancer; however, Mino's Peruvian culture controls the amount of tobacco, and for centuries has used its fresh and dried leaves, smoke, and oil for healings.

At Shabeta's Healing Garden, Mino begins his healing process with ceremonies to the tobacco seeds he will use in healing, followed by honoring the planting and harvesting seasons. The seeds are blessed and dedicated to healing and when the plants are harvested they have the same dedication, intention, and prayer. He emphasizes the connection with plants by suggesting praying and talking to them and he reminds me of my mother's love of plants; she would ask their forgiveness when pulling or cutting parts of them for medicine or food.

Mino squeezes the juice from the fresh tobacco plant and uses it for skin rashes. He recommends that women consider tobacco for hot steam sitz baths for painful menstrual problems. He suggests boiling and adding tobacco to the three plants described earlier by Bernadette (Calendula, Dandelion, and Mullein) and using the blends in a bath, then self-drying without using a towel. The tobacco helps the three plants bring out their healing properties. He uses tobacco smoke for a limpia in order to adjust and remove unwanted energies and to connect to the spiritual world.

**Conclusion:** Like the curandero Laurencio Nuñez mentioned earlier, Mino is a gentle spiritual healer whose ancient tradition of using tobacco for his holistic healings is being kept alive. Mino's work follows in a long tradition of medicinal and spiritual uses for tobacco in the Americas (Struthers, 2004).

# CHAPTER 13

# Herbal Smoke for Healing

I met Dr. Monica Lucero a few years ago and was impressed with how she was able to blend traditional curanderismo into her training as a certified Doctor of Oriental Medicine, since many of the medicinal plants and some cultural aspects are shared. In this book, we have explored the similarities of Mediterranean, Native-American, African, and Afro-Caribbean traditional medicine to that of curanderismo. Dr. Lucero has been able to use the rich Asian healing traditions to enrich the medicine of her Hispanic ancestors. As a community volunteer, she has helped those in need by teaching them how to to grow their own food, use it nutritiously, and to understand the importance of traditional medicine. Dr. Lucero serves the community as a traditional medicine advocate with the **Remembering Ancestors, Inspiring Culture, Empowering Self (RAICES)** program. She is practicing acupuncture and traditional medicine in the communities of Los Lunas and Albuquerque and practices at the Red Root Acupuncture and Herbs clinic.

In this chapter on "Herbal Smoke for Healing," Dr. Lucero demonstrates the healing properties of moxibustion, a therapy from Chinese traditional medicine, also known as moxa. This healing method consists of burning dried Mugwort, *Artemisia vulgaris*, known as *Estafiate* in Spanish, and placing it over certain acupuncture points of the body. The moxa is prepared by rolling the Mugwort plant into a cigar-shaped herbal stick, or the plant can be placed in a moxa box, lit and utilized on the afflicted part of the body so that the smoke and heat of the Mugwort invigorates the blood and enters the blocked body channels. It is believed that this practice originated in Northern China and Mongolia where moxa was adapted to the cold weather conditions.

In earlier years, a tool was used to remove the wool-like material from the Mugwort plant. Now, an electric blender breaks up the plant wool much quicker in order to roll it into a moxa stick.

Dr. Lucero uses the Mugwort plant smoke for a diagnosis to determine what meridian points need to be unblocked and to help induce a smoother flow of blood. She compares the moxa smoke to that of the copal resin used by curanderos(as) and the white sage smoke popular with Native-American healers, in order to cleanse the spirit and balance the energies.

She mentions that there are about fifty types of moxa, with the two main forms being direct and indirect. The direct moxa is practiced by advanced practitioners, mostly in China and is applied directly on the skin at an acupuncture point. It burns until the skin blisters and scars after it heals.

Figure 13.1 Dr. Lucero uses the Mugwort plant smoke, moxa, on the meridian points, while the moxa box remains on Tom's back.

Dr. Lucero uses the indirect technique where she places a cigar-like moxa near the acupuncture point in order to heat the skin and treat kidney deficiencies or a lack of energy. She places a layer of salt over the umbilicus (belly button) and burns a cone of moxa over the salt, since the salt spreads the warms and burns, while the Mugwort smoke and steam penetrates the skin. This therapy is also used for incontinence and loose stools.

Dr. Lucero states that in earlier years, practitioners would heat a needle and insert it in the body. Nowadays, the acupuncture needle goes into the skin, and afterward, the moxa heats the needle and is used for body knots or areas that need to draw energy. Other types of moxa are the smokeless ones for allergies, and the liquids, which are heated with a lamp to give warmth and heal pain. Because the regular moxa should not be used on the face, there is a special moxa stick that can be used in order to open the nasal passages.

Dr. Lucero demonstrated the use of a moxa box on Dr. Tom Chávez, who is himself a practitioner of traditional medicine. This wooden box is about four by twelve inches with a slide lid and a screen in the bottom. Dried Mugwort wool is burned and placed inside the box, closed, and placed on the back of the body to alleviate muscular, arthritic, or rheumatic pain. The box with the plant smoke and heat is left on the body for a few minutes according to the heat tolerance of the person, and then moved to other locations that need attention.

**Conclusion:** Dr. Lucero has developed a positive reputation in the Albuquerque region for her caring and generosity in working with patients. She is unique in combining her many years of studying Chinese traditional medicine with her ancestral knowledge of curanderismo. She is a strong advocate of using moxa smoke to treat a number of ailments and reminds us of a quote from Dr. Yes, one of her professors: "One cone of moxa is worth ten acupuncture needles".

# CHAPTER 14
# Creating Sacred Spaces for Healing

During my teenage years, I spent some of my summers at the family ranch. The nearest neighbor lived about three miles away and the closest small community was at a distance of about fifty miles. This isolation allowed me to enjoy the quiet and gave me space to think, meditate, and to create a sacred space in the *arroyo*, which was a dried creek with seasonal rain that kept it green and full of wild local plants and flowers. My favorite time for this sacred space was early in the morning or late afternoon when I would lie on the grass and enjoy the aroma of the flowers, and occasionally see rabbits, *javelinas* (wild boar), deer, and wild turkeys. The sacred space allowed me personal time to begin the day with a positive attitude and full of energy and would calm me down in the afternoons to prepare me for a good night's rest.

After the summer, I would go to our small community and enjoy my family's sacred space, which was an altar in the corner of our living room. Although this was the family altar, my mother was its owner and caretaker. She would decide what was placed in this sacred space such as a couple of candles, a crucifix, a container with holy water, plastic flowers, an image of the Virgin of Guadalupe (patron saint of Mexico), a photo of the Pope, the late President Robert F. Kennedy, and my two uncles who were killed in the world wars. This sacred place was used during the family prayer night that consisted of reciting the rosary, praying for someone's needs, or being in the space for personal meditation. Most of our neighbors had similar sacred spaces or altars in various rooms of their homes such as a bedroom, a special room in the back of house, or in the living room. When visiting my friends, I would always check out the items on their altar and return home to share them with my mother to see if we could add something new to our sacred space.

My wife, Nieves, grew up in Brownsville, located on the coastal tip of South Texas next to the Mexican border town of Matamoros on the the Gulf of Mexico, and she spent many days on the beach in South Padre Island. The sand and ocean environment became her sacred space. Even now, most of our vacations are on a beach in Cancun or Cabo San Lucas, Mexico, and she is always spending an early morning in her sacred space, sitting on the sanding beach enjoying the sunrise and sounds of the ocean waves.

**Figure 14.1** A healer's sacred space contains a number of symbolical elements.

Rita and Tonita, spiritual healers whom you already know from previous chapters, discuss the creation of a sacred space (an altar) that they create with natural elements, as part of a temazcal sweat lodge experience, which includes a ceremony to honor the four directions. The space is similar to an altar used as part of a healing therapy in one of their clinics. They encourage others to create their own sacred space within their home, or as a community project, in order to bring people together. During a two-week participation at the annual Smithsonian Folklife Festival, Rita and Tonita asked a few of the almost one million visitors to the festival to organize a sacred space every morning when the festival opened its doors. A diverse group of visitors of all ages and from different countries organized the altar using many of the elements from nature that Rita will be demonstrating. This sacred space was enjoyed on a daily bases by the hundreds of people that stopped by the altar and meditated for a few moments before visiting our exhibit on curanderismo and the presentations we delivered to hundreds of visitors.

The following are the elements from Mother Nature that Rita and Tonita use in preparing their Sacred space:

1. **Seeds:** Rita states that seeds represent our daily bread. The seeds selected for the sacred space represent the region, environment, or culture, such as the sacred wild rice that was given to her by a group of Native Americans from the state of Minnesota.

2. **Water:** A container of pure or holy water is part of the sacred space, since water represent purity not only in Christianity but also in Hinduism, Judaism, Islam, Taoism, and other world religions. It is considered an aspect of the feminine just as fire is associated with the masculine.

3. **Corn:** Tonita tells us that there are basically seven colors of corn with a meaning for each color; I have seen her using different colors of corn such as white, yellow, and black to represent the different forms of human beings.

4. **Plants:** There are a number of plants and flowers that are placed in the sacred space to represent the food and traditional medicinal plants that we use to heal us.

5. **Incense Burner, *Peliacate, Copal:*** The sahumerio, the kerchief, called a *peliacate*, and the resin incense named copal, are discussed in the chapters on limpias, and are part of most healer's sacred space.

6. **Obsidian Stone:** This black shiny volcanic stone is considered a smoking mirror that reflects us to ourselves and connects us with our ancestors.
   It is described in the previous chapter on, "Healing through Sound."

7. **Other Elements:** Other elements that Rita and Tonita use in their sacred space are the quartz crystal for power and energy, the feather that can also be used for a limpia, the rattles for the sound of water, a bit of mother earth and figurines of sea animals such as the turtle and airanimals like birds.

**Conclusions:** Sacred spaces are inspirational and spiritual and found in all world religions and traditions. Rita and Tonita remind us to use personal items in order to create our own sacred and meaningful space. In my earlier years, my sacred space was an *arroyo* creek in the family ranch, my wife's was and is the beach, and my mother's and my family's space was an altar in our living room. Rita and Tonita continue creating sacred spaces almost on a daily basis as part of their healing and spiritual life.

Figure 14.2 Rita and Tonita create a separate space similar to the ones used in Temazcal sweat lodges and in other ceremonies.

# CHAPTER 15
# Native American Feather Healing

I met Robert (Bob) Vetter a few years ago and was surprised that someone from Long Island, New York, would travel to the University of New Mexico to learn about curanderismo. I soon discovered that he had been conducting fieldwork in the area of spirituality and healing among the Southern Plains tribes since the early 1980s, while he was in the process of completing his Master's Degree from the University of Oklahoma in Anthropology. After visiting with Bob, I learned that he was adopted into families from the Cheyenne, Kiowa, and Comanche tribes and that his adopted grandfather was the last medicine man of the Comanches, Oliver Pahdopony. He co-authored a book, *Big Bow: The Spiritual Life and Teachings of a Kiowa Family* with his adopted Kiowa uncle, Richard Tartsah, Sr. (2012). As President of "**Journeys into American Indian Territory**," he has contributed to educating the public firsthand on traditional teachings and contemporary lifeways of Native Americans. It was a Cheyenne elder and father figure, Moses Starr, (his adopted father in the Cheyenne way) who mentored and taught Bob the use of feathers for healing. A well-known local curandera and a dear friend who passed away a few years ago, Elena Avila, was another of Bob's teachers who taught him the use of feathers as used in limpias.

Bob has been able to compare curanderismo to the traditional medicine of the Native Americans of the Southern Plains. He begins his presentation on the use of feathers for limpias by stating how feathers are used in the Native American Church, a religion with elements of Christianity and Shamanism, that was started in the late 1800s in the state of Oklahoma after *peyote* was introduced to the Southern Great Plains tribes. *Peyote* is a cactus with psychoactive alkaloids that has been used for rituals and medicine for centuries by some of the indigenous tribes of Mexico also. The Native American church believes *peyote* is a gift from God. The church encourages its members to abstain from the use of alcohol, promotes values such as being faithful to a spouse, telling the truth, taking care of family, working to support family, and praying for the sick and for peace.

As a member of the Native American Church, Bob uses the feather as part of the all-night ceremony inside the tepee. In addition to prayers, singing and taking the sacramental *peyote* communion, feathers are taken out of the individual peyote boxes after the midnight water rite.

Bob describes his *peyote* wooden box where he keeps his sacred tools for ceremonies and limpias, such as a bundle of different colored feathers attached to a beaded dowel and a single Bustard tail feather that comes from Australia. In addition to the feathers, he mentions the items on a sacred space altar he has created that includes a gourd rattle, an incense burner, copal incense resin, sage, sweetgrass, and Florida water. Most of these elements will be used in his limpia and others are utilized with different ceremonies or other types of spiritual cleansings.

The following are two limpias Bob demonstrated on his wife Maddi, and another two on me, using copal incense smoke in combination with the feather for all his spiritual cleansings.

**Limpia on Maddi:** In the first feather cleansing, Bob burns the copal incense in a sahumerio burner and constantly uses a single feather to gather the copal smoke in order to smudge Maddi, beginning with her head and going down to her feet, since women are smudged from top, down. He constantly sweeps her aura using a fast tapping motion about six inches from her body, and not touching it, since he is smoothing her energetic field. In his second limpia, Bob stirs Maddi's energy by quickly moving the feather around her aura from head to toe. In the next step, he slows down the motion of the feather with a gentle tap-like motion away from her body in order to create a protective barrier around her energetic field. In the last step, he rubs Florida water, (fragrant water considered a "spiritual food") on his hands, which are used to sweep her entire energetic field, but not touching her body. This again, creates a protective barrier around the essence of her aura. Bob hugs Maddi as a sign of gratitude for allowing him to perform this feather limpia.

**Figure 15.1** Bob uses the feather, copal smoke, and a prayer for a Native American cleansing on Cheo.

**Limpia on Cheo:** My limpia was similar to Maddi's except that Bob started with a single feather at my feet and moved to my head, since for men the spiritual cleansing is bottom to top. Before completing the limpia with the feather, he taps both of my open hands and my heart area. In the second limpia, Bob takes the bundle of feathers, instead of one, and begins to fan the feathers in a tapping motion throughout my body's aura while constantly gathering the copal smoke with the feather.

The limpia was in combination with a special prayer asking the Creator for special blessing and protections. This is part of Bob's prayer, "Creator, I ask that you be with me today as I pray to bless Cheo that, through me, your power will go into him…I pray that you put a shield around him and that with the smoke and feather, he will be protected…" *Excerpt reprinted by permission of Bob Vetter.*

**Conclusion:** Bob mentions that we can find feathers while walking or we can purchase them through the internet, such as those of the macaw, pheasant or bustard. Some, such as the sacred eagle feather, are illegal to purchase or own. However, feathers are all around us and those that we find can be perceived as gifts from the sky that can be used to help us and others. The birds can be considered spiritual guides whose feathers we borrow to do good. Bob has been able to use his knowledge of Native American healing and that of curanderismo to develop a unique bicultural limpia experience of both cultures. Recently, he constructed a Mexican temazcal sweat lodge in Long Island, New York, and continues working with healers from Mexico in order to strengthen his knowledge of healing the body, mind, and spirit.

# CHAPTER 16

# Bonesetter (*Huesero*)

As a child, my father, who grew up in a farm, would tell stories about the huesero, bonesetter, such as the one about the time his cousin fell from a horse and fractured his ankle and foot. The nearest physician was about three hours away and many times he would make house-calls and would not be in his clinic for a few days; however, there was a huesero in the neighboring ranch who had learned the art of bone setting from a relative in Mexico. Therefore, they took his screaming cousin who was in excruciating pain to see the man. As my father recalled, "The huesero was a small grey haired man of about 80 years of age and his clinic was a tiny special room in the back of his home with only a twin size bed, two chairs, and a number of human skeletal and muscular charts pinned on the wall." My relative was placed on the bed and to calm him down, he was quickly given a special tonic that my dad thought smelled like *tequila*. Everyone was to leave the room and after about four hours they returned to find the cousin fast asleep with his foot bandaged. After a few months, the relative was working, riding horses, and pain free. A few years later, the same relative suffered another injury and went to a hospital where he had an X-ray. After examining the image of his foot, the physician asked the man which hospital and doctor had performed an excellent job of repairing his fracture and the response was, "A huesero did it."

Nowadays, the huesero has practically disappeared from this country. This profession was around before the osteopaths, chiropractors, and physical therapists, and was done without formal medical qualifications. The huesero learned by apprenticing with someone else or was self-taught by reading and experimenting with muscles and bones. This is the case with Agustín Pérez from Mexico City who learned the profession from his grandfather, Maurelio, and his father, Roberto. Agustin has developed a reputation in a city of more than twenty million people and is one of the very few practicing hueseros in this metropolitan area. Although Agustin sets dislocated bones, in this demonstration he will perform running cupping, ventosas corridas, similar to the Rita's therapy as mentioned in the chapter on **Fire Cupping**. The difference in Agustin's style of cupping is that he sprays alcohol in the glass in order to create a stronger pull on the skin that impacts the muscles, nerves, and tendons. His demonstration of the therapy is on Dr. Tom Chávez. This cupping session addresses the sciatic nerves that causes severe pain from the lower back to the hips, buttocks, and legs. He will also do a brief therapy to clear empacho, intestinal blockage that has been discussed in the previous chapter by Tana and on espanto (extreme fright), which is similar to the chapter on susto (fright) presented by Rita. The following are the steps Agustin takes in his demonstration:

1.  **Preparation:** Agustín begins this demonstration by gaining Tom's confidence and relaxing the muscles on his neck and back while also opening the skin pores. While Tom sits upright and shirtless on a chair, the huesero rubs on oil and massages his neck and back using a traditional sobada massage. The next step is to take a glass, spray alcohol inside, wipe the rims of the glass of the alcohol,

and to place a lit lighter under the glass in order to create a vacuum that will pull the skin up when the glass is placed on the body. Generally, Rita does not spraying the inside of the glass with alcohol and uses a lit alcohol soaked cotton ball to create a smaller amount of suction on the skin. Agustín does the running cupping on the base of the neck and shoulders and completes the therapy by rubbing alcohol in the area in order to close the skin pores. Before moving to another part of the body, he adjusts Tom's neck by twisting it to the left and right in order to pop the joints of the neck.

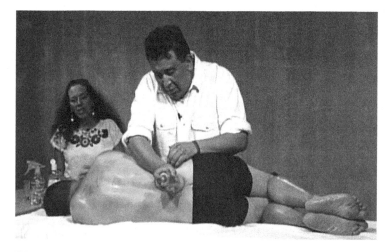

**Figure 16.1** Agustin, one of the last bonesetters, is demonstrating a running *ventosa* for Sciatica pain, on Tom.

2. **Sciatica Running Ventosas:** Tom is now asked to lay on the massage table face down and the huesero continues the same process in opening the pores with alcohol, rubbing oil on the legs and back, proceeded by doing a running cupping and following the sciatica nerve that aligns the spinal column. Then he moves to the hip area, backs of the knees, calves, and the soles and heels of the feet. The session is completed by closing the pores with alcohol.

3. **Empacho:** Agustin does a brief demonstration on how he addresses empacho, an intestinal blockage where food can accumulate or get stuck, causing constipation. Tom lies on his back and his abdomen is sprayed with oil, followed by a cupping on his lower abdomen in order to activate the digestive system. Then he moved to the areas of the colon, liver, and spleen in order to also activate them. Like the previous cuppings, he closed the pores with alcohol.

4. **Espanto:** His last demonstration is treating espanto, which is a more intense form of susto. In this simple but effective therapy, he asks Tom to call out his name three times while Agustín quickly, with open hands, brushes the front of his body from face to feet. The belief is that the huesero is sweeping away the negative vibrations that have caused the espanto symptoms of insomnia and anxiety. Agustin sprays alcohol on a small towel, places it on Tom's face, and asks him to inhale deeply and to exhale before removing it.

**Conclusion:** It was refreshing to learn that a huesero, practicing a tradition that has basically disappeared in this country, continues to follow the art of his ancestors in Mexico. Agustin's demonstration was on the sciatica nerve since it's a pain that most people around the world suffer from. I realized how diverse his treatments are since he also showed us how he treats empacho and espanto. These are therapies that are easy to learn and, if done correctly, can help in supporting family and friends. I was impressed with a comment made by Agustin, when he stated, "I can hear how the energy is expanding." Indeed, his three demonstrations of a running ventosa for sciatica, empacho, and espanto, dealt with balancing and "hearing" one's spirit and energy for a healthier body and mind.

# CHAPTER 17
# Mayan Traditional Healing

## 17.1 INTRODUCTION TO MAYAN TRADITIONAL MEDICINE

Chapter 17 is divided into two subchapters addressing Mayan acupuncture and abdominal massage. Sofia Salazar has been studying, practicing, and teaching traditional acupuncture for several years and has compared the Chinese approach to Mayan techniques. Alex Jackson has studied Mayan Abdominal Massage with one of the well-known healers of Belize, Rosita Arvigo.

I became interested in Mayan traditional medicine after a few trips to two Mexican states: Chiapas and Yucatan, where a large number of Mayans live. I went to Chiapas, which borders the country of Guatemala, a number of times with a professor and mentor, Dr. Stanley Bittinger. On our trips to the communities of San Cristobal de las Casas and the Lacandon jungle, I met a number of Mayans who were knowledgeable in herbal medicine and traditional rituals that had been passed down through several generations. The blending of the Mayan and Christian religion was incorporated into some of their rituals that involved prayer, plants, copal resin incense, candles, and other elements that are common in curanderismo.

A second state with a rich Mayan population and culture was Yucatan, where I spent some time in the capital city of Merida, with a group of Mayan healers and herbalist, at an international conference on traditional medicine. During the conference, I was invited to a traditional sweat lodge, the temazcal that has been discussed in a previous chapter. I also became interested in the **Chaya, *Cnidoscolus chayamansa*** plant, also called Spinach Tree, after a presentation by a Mayan professor and healer on its properties and cures. I learned that that his plant is very high in vitamins and minerals, with a concentration of potassium and calcium, and is an excellent antioxidant. The Mayan professor told me that he had done research on the medicinal properties of **Chaya** and that it controlled diabetes, if boiled and taken daily as drinking water. I asked for some cuttings of the plant, brought it to Texas A&M University-Kingsville, where I worked at the time, and asked a colleague, Dr. Joseph Kuti, if he would do research on the effectiveness of Chaya on diabetes. He did the research and published the results indicating that the plant did indeed control type-2 diabetes.

What I learned from my visits to Chiapas and Yucatan was that the large indigenous Mayan culture has maintained strong ancient traditional medicinal values. With their herbal medicine and rituals they have kept alive the holistic approach to healing for hundreds of years and incorporated mind, body, spirit, and religion. I was impressed with the Mayan curanderos called *ah-men* and how they would provide all types of services to their communities, serving the roles of a priest, doctor,and counselor.

Mayan traditional medicine is holistic in nature and addresses illness via a connection with the plants, frequent use of temazcal sweat lodges, and uses the techniques of a huesero. It has also kept alive other healing arts such as midwifery. However, in this chapter, we will only be discussing Mayan acupuncture and abdominal massage therapies that are still being utilized in the Mayan culture.

## 17.2 MAYAN ACUPUNCTURE

Reyna Salazar Sotelo is known as Sofia and she began her profession as a trained biologist in Cuernavaca. After studying traditional Mayan and Chinese acupuncture, she was one of the founders of the Community Center for Human Development. She is now a practitioner and professor of acupuncture and medicinal plants, and trains traditional healers from her Mexican state and region.

Sofia begins her introduction of Mayan acupuncture by stating that it borrowed many of its techniques from Chinese traditional medicine; however, we are not sure about possible connections between ancient Chinese and Mayan cultures because of vast differences between these countries. Sofia works with the Chinese concept of *yin* and *yang* and relates it to Mayan traditions of balancing hot and cold medicine. The *yin* is considered feminine and negative while the yang is masculine and positive. Both complement each other.

Instead of using the Chinese thin, sterile needles, the Mayan ancestors would use the spine needle of the Maguey plant, or the spine needles of fish, and would sterilize them with garlic, a natural antibiotic. Sofia discusses some of the traditional acupuncture points practiced by the Mayans, which are similar to Chinese practices:

1. **Point between the Eyebrows:** Mayan elders believed that the point between the eyebrows and above the bridge of the nose should be punctured at least once in your lifetime. This is done in order to remove a bad essence placed there at birth and the goal is to bleed the point and leave the needle a few minutes to remove the hot wind stored in the body, which could be the cause of ailments. This is also done in Chinese medicine. The point is known as the *yintang* and is important because the blood of the head runs through this point, which is connected to ailments associated with the nose and head.

2. **Point on top of the Head:** Mayan grandparents would place a needle on top of the head close to the forehead, and would allow it to bleed. The belief was that this would unblock the person's spirit. In Chinese acupuncture this point addresses asthma and headaches.

3. **Point on the Abdomen:** In order to check the body heat, Sofia places her hands on the the patient's abdomen. She then inserts three needles on the abdomen in the form of a triangle close to the navel area. The objective is to remove trapped heat around the abdomen area that could be impacting the digestive system.

4. **Moxa on the Feet:** Sofia touches the feet and discovers that they are cold and decides to use moxibustion or moxa to warm them. This therapy was demonstrated by Dr. Monica Lucero in a previous chapter and the concept is to warm the feet with a cigar-like herbal stick of dried Mugwort, which brings heat down to the feet. This allows the flow of energy, or *Qi*, in Chinese traditional medicine. The hot herbal stick on the feet produces a soft heat that moves the blood from the feet and legs to the head, and brings the heat from the top of the body to the feet, in order circulate the *Qi* energy and bring balance to the body.

5. **Scraping the Arm:** In order to improve blood circulation, detoxification, and a good energy flow, Sofia applies olive oil to the patient's upper body and uses a smooth edged round instrument to gently scrape, with short brisk strokes, the patient's forearm. The amount of tension and muscle tightness tells Sofia how much heat is trapped in this part of the body and how scraping will help. This therapy is done on other parts of the body, especially the back, where all of the organs are represented. Chinese traditional medicine calls this therapy *Gua Sha* and is a treatment mainly used for pain, stress, fatigue and to restore the flow of *Qi* to the area.

**Figure 17.1** Sophia is using Mayan acupuncture to remove heat from the digestive system.

6. **Comparing Mayan to Chinese Acupuncture:** Sofia mentions that Mesoamerican medicine has more acupuncture points than the 365 recognized by the Chinese; however, the points to calm emotions, remove heat from the stomach, and to regulate intestinal movement, are the same in both cultures. The principal of applying hot and cold to illnesses is also the same in Mayan and Chinese medicine. Both cultures have more similarities in acupuncture techniques than differences.

**Conclusion:** In this chapter, we are able to appreciate Mayan traditional medicine with an emphasis on acupuncture. We have compared it to the many Chinese acupuncture points in the body and have discovered that many are the same. Sofia has demonstrated these points in the face, head, and abdomen, with minor differences such as the Mayan point between the eyebrows for removing the bad essence from birth. The Mayan concept of relating illnesses to a balance of hot and cold is similar to the ancient Chinese belief in *yin* and *yang*, where opposites complement one another. What is still a puzzle is how these connections and similarities between both ancient cultures developed hundreds of years ago.

## 17.3  MAYAN ABDOMINAL MASSAGE

Alex Jackson grew up in Albuquerque, New Mexico, and relocated to Kansas City, Missouri, where he established the **Centered Spirit—Cultural and Holistic Center** to serve patients in traditional medicine, specializing in Mayan Abdominal Massage. Recently, after years of study with Rita Navarrete, he added a Mexican sweat lodge/temazcal as part of his healing therapies. He also studied with two other internationally known master healers. One was the late Elena Avila who was born in El Paso and practiced in Albuquerque. She started her career as a registered nurse and worked in psychiatry before becoming a curandera specializing in limpias and traditional counseling, or *platicas*. The second healer, Rosita Arvigo, was born in Chicago and trained as an herbalist and Doctor of Naturopathy. She later moved to Belize in Central America where she trained with a well-known Mayan shaman healer, Don Elijio. She directs a public clinic, ***Ix Chel* Wellness Center**, in San Ignacio, Cayo, Belize. Rosita has also developed **The Arvigo Techniques of Maya Abdominal Therapy,** which she teaches around the world.

Over the last few decades, Alex has developed his own techniques for Maya Abdominal Massage, based on ancient principles in the Maya healing traditions. He will demonstrate and discuss one version of these techniques in this chapter. In his practice, he offers traditional ways of healing the body and spirit through the abdomen, therapies that he learned from many traditional healers in Central America and Mexico, beginning with Rosita Arvigo. Alex believes that proper balance is needed in the core to resolve many physical ailments and emotional traumas and realizes that the abdomen is the doorway to achieving health and a "centered spirit."

In his demonstration of Maya Abdominal Massage, he begins by stating that one of the most commonly overlooked organs of our body is the abdomen, which houses our digestive and reproductive systems. We may get a massage for back, neck, arm, and leg pains, but overlook our abdomen. When our abdomen gets tight or there is discomfort, we may take a medication or change our diet, but neglect to massage it like we have done to other parts of our body. The abdomen is a complete living and breathing organism. Alex begins his treatment by asking the patient to relax and places his hands on the abdomen in order to connect with the patient, feel their energy and breathing. Alex believes that breathing is the most important thing to observe in a patient, since it is the life force that connects the body, beginning with the abdomen and moving to the rest of the body.

Connecting with the patient is important, such as asking how they feel, if there is pain, discomfort, or tenderness and also what emotions they are experiencing during the massage, since emotional stress impacts the various organs. Alex believes that stressful emotions impact our organs including those within our stomach and that the healer should make the patient aware of this relationship between the emotion and the ailment. He reminds us that his curanderismo-based abdominal therapy is holistic and incorporates the physical with the emotional elements. The following are Alex's treatments as practiced by the Mayan tradition:

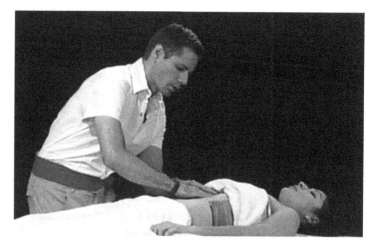

**Figure 17.2** Alex's Mayan Abdominal massage on Sonai addresses several problems with the digestive and reproductive systems.

1. **Problems in the Diaphragm:** Before beginning his abdominal massage, if a patient comes to Alex with digestive issues or acid reflux as a consequence of stomach acid moving from the diaphragm to the esophagus, they are asked to talk about any stress they are dealing with. He realizes the importance of the diaphragm, which can contract around the vena cava and aorta, thus restricting proper flow of blood.

2. **Problems in the Esophagus:** According to Alex, "Emotional stress has an effect of almost literally pinching the esophagus." A simple way to relieve the esophagus is simply to massage the diaphragm. The Mayan traditional masseuse re-uses a small amount of oil and gently pushes down on the solar plexus, which has a complex network of nerves, and continues massaging down to the navel area. At times, the healer will feel a slight bump, blockage, or soft pulse. If the patient's stress is not controlled, the blockage worsens. Alex tells us that the Mayan sobador/a can alleviate the problem by gently pressing and massaging this pulse, bump, or blockage.

3. **Problems with the Liver:** During the abdominal massage, Alex moves his hands toward the liver and, at times, feels tightness or tenderness around this area. He talks to the patient about any frustration or anger issues, realizing that it is associated with the liver, especially suppressed or extreme anger. As with the Maya, it is also a part of traditional Chinese medicine that anger causes the energy flow to be blocked and Alex believes that he can unblock it with his abdominal massage. Chinese traditional medicine may use acupuncture needles to allow a better flow of energy.

4. **Problems with the Colon:** When Alex massages the lower abdomen around the colon, he may feel some tightness and will ask the patient how they are feeling. He continues massaging the right side for possible congestion around the colon that could cause empacho. Chronic or frequent constipation is related to stress that needs to be purged and eliminated. While massaging the abdomen, he continues asking the patient how they are feeling so that any accumulated stress can leave the body. The result is an awareness and release of any fascia restrictions that were affecting the colon and causing constipation.

**Conclusion:** Alex informs us that in curanderismo, if a patient has tightness on the left side of the body, it is associated with feminine energy while the right side is aligned with masculinity. This philosophy reminds me of the Mesoamerican concept of Ometeotl, dual cosmic energy, and the Chinese *yin* that represents the feminine, while the *yang* the masculine, and the belief that opposites complement each other. Alex tells us that after completing the Mayan abdominal massage, the patient may regain movements of peristalsis (tension and relaxation of digestion canals) within the abdomen. Breathing is also easier, and there is less tenderness and sensitiveness around the abdomen. Some patients report tingling in their arms and legs, which means that there is renewed blood circulation and nerve flow to that part of the body. He completes most of his traditional abdominal massages with a spiritual limpia using plants. He often uses the aromatic Rosemary and sweeps the body with the herbs, especially the abdomen, while reciting a prayer. Alex, says, "Many times, it is normal for the patient to experience a connection between the physical and the emotional." That is why his favorite quote is, "Awareness is healing."

# CHAPTER 18
# Introduction to Traditional Body Work

I n a previous chapter, we learned about the role of the huesero, a profession that has disappeared in the United States and is becoming extinct in Mexico. Huesero Agustín Perez, from Mexico City, discusses and demonstrates how he learned his profession, without formal training, from his father and grandfather. He shows us how he worked with sciatica nerve pain that starts in the lower back and travels down to the foot. He uses deep fire cupping to manipulate the nerves and relieve the pain. He also demonstrates a brief treatment for empacho and espanto.

Even though, the huesero has practically disappeared in the United States and Mexico, this category of healer has survived in other countries such as Japan, where they are known as *sekkotsus,* or China where they are called *die-das*. These bonesetters set broken, fractured or dislocated bones, manipulate muscular problems, and perform therapeutic massages. In Mexico, they also offer healing rituals such as the curing of susto and limpias.

In the following two subchapters on body and spinal adjustment, two traditional healers do a treatment similar to that of the huesero, and at times are called by this title. Roberto Suárez and the late Felipa Sánchez are traditional healers from Mexico and part of my summer two-week class on curanderismo. In addition to teaching their skills in my class, they have traveled to other parts of the United States to conduct short training classes and services for a number of patients. Sadly, Felipa passed away on her return trip from Albuquerque, New Mexico to her community in Mexico. In addition to body adjustments and alignments, their skills are diverse in several other areas of traditional medicine. Their speciality is working as what could be called "traditional chiropractors" since chiropractic therapy is fairly new and did not exist during the time that the art of the hueseros was developing.

## 18.1 BODY ADJUSTMENT

Roberto Suárez apprentice with a well-known traditional healer from the Mexican state of Guerrero. He is a curandero with a clinic that specializes in different methods of healing such as sports adjustments, auricular therapy, pediatric massage, flower essence/oils for the back, acupuncture, and herbalism. He has been involved in constructing a temazcal in the community of Los Lunas, New Mexico.

Roberto has asked me to be his patient, in order to demonstrate a total body adjustment and bring balance, which simply means to help in creating a restful relaxed body without pain or discomfort. He takes the following steps in performing the body adjustment:

1. **Analyzing/Aligning the Body:** He begins analyzing the body by manipulating the feet, in a way that is similar to reflexology or acupressure. Both reflexology and acupuncture use pressure on certain points of the foot, which are connected to other parts of the body and relax muscular tension, helping with swelling and pain. Roberto touches my toes, and moves and pulls them

while placing some pressure, since the feet are the base that support the weight of our body. He is also relaxing and stretching the ligaments, nerves, and tendons. This exercise helps align the bones in order for the muscles to be placed in the correct space. In working with the feet, Roberto notices some discomfort in the hips and fatigue in the backbone. He moves the toes and the heel, and activates them by slowly rotating the foot. Roberto reminds me that carrying body weight wears down the muscles and bones in our heels

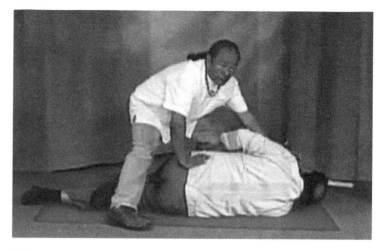

**Figure 18.1** Roberto adjusts the lower body with movement of the hip area.

and causes fatigue and pain, even the painful *plantar fasciitis*. Finally, he holds the feet and pulls my leg in order to adjust the hip. All this time he is communicating with me on what he is doing.

2. **Adjusting the Lower Body:** My lower body is adjusted by asking me to lie on my side with the left leg stretched and the upper right leg bent, and placing my hands on my side. In this comfortable position, the body begins to re-adjust itself without any pain other than what the patient may already have. Roberto stands over my body, bends and places one hand on my hip and the other one on my shoulder, and pushes each side in opposite directions in order to adjust the back and hip. This adjustment movement is repeated on my other side.

3. **Adjusting the Spinal Column:** I am asked to lie on my stomach with arms by my side. Roberto places his hands on the base of my spine in order to feel if there's fatigue or tiredness and to check the condition of the spinal column. With open hands, he gently pushes up and down each side of the spinal column, followed by doing the same procedure using two fingers, directly on the spinal column. He was checking for any abnormalities on the back and the spinal column. He reminded me that that our skeletal structure does not need much force or strength for adjustments, and that with gentleness they will find their correct alignment.

4. **Adjusting the Upper Body:** I lie on my back and Roberto begins by working on my hands and arms. He takes my hand and pulls the fingers followed by rotating the wrist and pulling my arm for an upper body adjustment. He feels tears and weakness on the hands and wrists as a possible result of carrying a heavy briefcase and luggage, as well as playing golf on a regular basis. Roberto is correct since I experience constant pain and weakness in my wrists. He adjusts my shoulders by a gentle pull and manipulation of the arm and this same technique is used for dislocated shoulders. He kneels in front of my head and places his hands at the base of the neck, asking me to close my mouth while he pulls on the back on the neck.

5. **Knee Adjustment:** The last adjustment is the knee and Roberto tells me that many patients come to him with tears in the meniscus (knee tissue) caused by turning the knee quickly, or a fall. He asks me to bend the knee, places two thumbs at the base of the knee, and stretches it with a gentle pull.

**Conclusion:** I was glad that Roberto demonstrated his skills of body adjustment on me since I was suffering some body and knee discomfort. It could have been because of some exercise or my weekend golf games. After his therapy, I was pain-free and had a good amount of energy for the rest of the week. The treatment was gentle and Roberto's constant communication relaxed me and allowed me to trust him. At his clinic in Mexico, Roberto is able to serve the community, where people do not have the economic means to see chiropractors or physicians. He charges a minimal fee or none at all, depending on the patient's ability to pay. He also incorporates other techniques that may include a spiritual limpia, or a medicinal plant, in order to provide a holistic approach to healing.

## 18.2  SPINAL ADJUSTMENT

Felipa Maria Magdalena Sánchez was a dear friend who passed away on a return trip from Albuquerque, New Mexico, to her village outside the community of San Felipe del Progreso in the state of Mexico (the region by which Mexico City is found). I spent many hours with Felipa during her trips to visit our community at the invitation of a well-known local herbalist, Maclovia Sánchez de Zamora, who offered Felipe a clinic attached to her herb store called Ruppe Drugs, founded in 1883. Felipa was a gifted faith healer of many talents such as having visions and the ability to see beyond the physical. She was religious, combining prayer with many of her native traditional healings. She was called a bonesetter, but actually trained under a chiropractor for several years and was versed in anatomy and the science of the muscular system. She would tell me stories of growing up in a small Mazahua native community and practicing several ceremonies such as Day of the Dead, New Fire, and Offering to Water. She was proud of her native ceremonial center founded to honor and preserve the Mazahua native culture and history. I will miss my friend and mentor, Felipa, and feel that she is still healing in the spirit world and, in many ways, reminds me of my teacher, Chenchito.

Before her demonstration of a spinal adjustment, Felipe mentioned that in addition to adjusting the spinal column, she would work on the nervous system in order to activate the entire body and provide a holistic healing. The following are the steps Felipa took in demonstrating her body adjustment:

1.  **Analyzing the Body:** After asking the patient to lie on a floor mat face down, Felipa performs a "human spiritual X-ray" by sweeping the body from head to toe using her opened hands, about six inches away from the body. When she gets to the feet, Felipa realizes that they are not the same length and states, "The reason for uneven legs could be the result of a fall, an injury, or lifting a heavy object. This also causes much tiredness."

2.  **Adjusting the Hips:** In order to adjust the uneven leg, Felipa manipulates the head of the femur bone that connects to the pelvic hip joint. She uses both hands to push on the upper buttock hip area in order to correct the head of the femur bone, and moves and pulls from the feet in order to complete the adjustment. After this is done, Felipa shows us how both legs are now equal in length.

3.  **Adjusting the Ribs:** By feeling the ribs, Felipa has discovered four floating ones. She corrects this by holding the patient's hand, rotating the arm and pulling in order to reset the ribs in the correct position. Felipa states, "This is like an operation without using a scalpel, with the person feeling better and without pain."

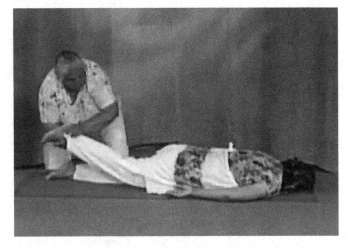

**Figure 18.2** Felipa pulls on the leg in order to make a hip adjustment.

4. **Adjusting and Activating Internal Organs:** Felipa adjusts the bladder by pushing back with open hands from the coccyx area, known as the tailbone, located at the bottom of the spine where there are ligaments, tendons, and muscles. She is also moving the nervous system in order to energize the kidneys by gently massage the kidney area. She moves to an acupressure area located on the back of the elbow and presses and massages this point three times, which allows oxygenation to the brain.

**Conclusion:** Felipa concludes her body adjustment by doing a spiritual limpia as a way of thanking the body for allowing her to adjust it. The patient is asked for comments and she mentioned a previous fall that twisted her ankle. She felt her hip was thrown off-balance. Without having disclosed this fall with Felipa before the spinal adjustment, Felipa was able to detect the problem and correct it. This was done through experience and intuition by a healer that has touched the lives of many people in two countries: the United States and Mexico. Even though she is no longer with us, her generosity, kindness, and healing will always be remembered. Her daugher is now receiving training and will follow in Felipa's path of helping others.

# CHAPTER 19
# Hydrotherapy (Healing with Water)

The therapeutic use of water is evident in ancient cultures such as Rome, Greece, Egypt, China, and Japan. In these cultures, not only were these waters used by royalty, but they were also available as public baths. We have all heard of popular hot Turkish baths and, in New Mexico, I often spend a few hours at a natural hot springs in a remote and beautiful region. These hot waters of Ojo Caliente date back thousands of years flowing through a volcanic aquifer and emptying in a number of pools such as a lithium, one for depression, an iron pool for the immune system, soda for the digestive system and an arsenic solution for skin conditions. After soaking in these waters for at least three hours, I feel energetic and my skin is like a baby's.

Rita has been able to create a simple method of using hydrotherapy without the expense of a therapeutic hot tub. Anyone can do her therapy with very little or no cost.

In her treatments, she uses hot or cold water, steam inhalations, water compresses, and water pressure, using a plain garden water hose. In combination with herbal teas, water has several properties that heal since it carries heat and energy and can dissolve minerals and salts.

The following are the ailments that are healed with water therapy as demonstrated by Rita with the help of Tonita:

1. **Infections and Tiredness: Calendula,** also called *mercadela, Calendula officinalis,* **English Marigold**, is an antiseptic, anti-inflammatory, and antifungal, that promotes healing. As a cooling plant, Rita prepares a tea for tired or infected feet and for toe fungus. A substitute herb is **Yerba Mansa***, Anemopsis californica,* **Swamp Root/Lizard Tail** or vinegar.
A foot bath with seawater is used for inflamed or tired feet, especially for those that walk all-day or whose jobs require them to be on their feet.

2. **Respiratory Ailments:** For respiratory ailments, a mixture of hot plants with hot water is used as a steam inhalation treatment, where a bowl of steaming water is mixed with the herbs or essential oils such as **Peppermint,** *Mentha piperita,* **Eucalyptus,** *Eucalyptus globulus,* **Myrtle,** *Myrtus communis,* **Rosemary,** *Rosmarinus officinalis.* The head is bent over the bowl with a towel covering the face and the steam is inhaled opening and clearing the nasal passages. Hot salves and ointments can be massaged into the face, around the sinus cavities in order to remove the energy and the

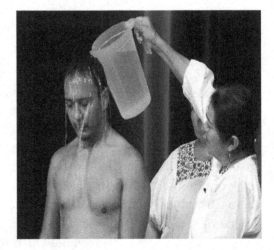

**Figure 19.1** Hydrotherapy can be utilized for a number of ailments, as demonstrated by Rita in the image above.

mucus. For an expectorant treatment, a hot wet towel is wrapped around a bundle of hot plants and made into a compress, which is pressed against the head, neck, chest, and lung areas. With the compress, Rita taps and massages the lymphatic system and continues tapping the back in order to stimulate the lungs and release more phlegm. After the treatment, she covers the body with a beach towel in order to keep it warm.

**Figure 19.2** Rita is stimulating blood circulation with the spray from the water hose.

3. **Detoxification:** In order to detox and energize the body, Rita or the patient can use a wet cold face towel to rub the body, stimulating and detoxifying it, beginning with the feet and moving up to the face. The towel compress should always be kept wet and the exfoliating rubbing should last from 20 to 30 minutes. After this is done, the patient is completely wrapped with a bed sheet, followed by a second wrap with a blanket. The patient is then taken outdoors and placed in the hot sun in order to provoke a sweat. The person is given an herbal tea and left to continue sweating. The rubbing of the lymphatic system combined with the wrapping of the body allows for a complete detox.

4. **Stimulating Blood Circulation:** Rita takes a garden water hose for a strong body spray, beginning with the sole of the feet, up the legs, the palms of the hands, up the arms, the head and the stomach, but not in the heart area. This process of stimulating the circulatory system is repeated a few times and is called a *piton*. A softer spray with the same process is called a *chorro*.

5. **Menopause symptoms:** In order to alleviate menopausal symptoms of hot flashes, night sweats, and insomnia, Rita recommends that a woman cover her bed with a plastic sheet and a dry beach towel. A small bed sheet is wet, squeezed, folded, and placed on the unclothed body between the legs, and up to her stomach. This is in order to balance the heat and energy of the body, improve the symptoms, and provide for a good night sleep.

6. **Yeast Infections:** For vaginal yeast infections or vaginitis, she recommends a sitz bath where a woman soaks in a bathtub with warm water mixed with herbs, a saline solution, or vinegar.

7. **Fever:** In order to lower the temperature of a fever, Rita suggests a simple remedy of placing a cold towel or compress on the head or over the eyes.

**Conclusion:** Water is part of life. It's free and can be a healing therapy with a minimum or no cost factor. Rita has shared with us how a simple water hose can be used to improve circulation of the body, a compress or steam from herbs for the respiratory system, and how a wet towel rubbing the lymphatic system can help detox our body. Our ancestors were able to do many of the simple traditional healing therapies that Rita has demonstrated to us. In our era, many of us are insured and rely on our medical system to alleviate our illnesses instead of empowering ourselves to take control of the health of our bodies. I believe that we can use good judgment and common sense about when to use traditional medicine to keep us healthy and have the judgment to seek medical services for serious illnesses.

# *Tonalli* Cleansing

I met Patricia Federico-Ruiz from Phoenix, Arizona, a few years ago. She has been to the summer curanderismo class a few times as a participant and as a presenter. She began her interest in traditional healing at a young age when she discovered her gift of empathy and intuitive experiences. Some call these gifts psychic but Patricia considers herself a servant of humanity with the purpose of easing the pain and suffering of others. She learned many of her healing skills from an aunt, a traditional sobadora who was well known in her community and region. After more than 20 years of experience with traditional healing, she now manages **My Madre Tierra** clinic located in a complex called "The Farm" at South Mountain, nestled by an ancient riverbed with naturally-rich soil within the Phoenix metropolitan area. Patricia offers a number of presentations and services including emotional healing, anxiety reduction and stress management. One of her patients quotes, "Patricia is extremely warm and caring, and one can feel her spiritual support throughout her healing sessions. She really cares, and I can feel that energy."

Patricia begins her demonstration by telling us that tonalli has different meanings in various cultures. Then we learn the steps Patricia takes in performing her tonalli cleansing:

1.  ***Tonalli* Meaning:** *Tonalli* comes from the Nahuatl word *tona,* which means heat, and is a symbol of the sun's warmth. The Aztecs believed that the tonalli was found in the hair and fontanelle (front) area of the skull and that this area provided energy for the person to grow and develop. This may explain why curanderos(as) still cure a *caida de mollera* or a fallen fontanelle in babies.

2.  **Preparing for the Tonalli Cleansing:** In her demonstration of healing the tonalli, Patricia asks the patient to lie face down on a massage table. Before beginning her treatment, she performs a spiritual/energetic cleansing on her using an herbal mist spray that she has prepared, called Madre Tierra Mist, that she developed through a vision she experienced in Mexico City. She uses the mist because she is in an indoor facility that is sensitive to smoke because of fire alarms. In a different setting she could use copal, white sage smudge stick smoke, water, cypress plants, or flowers. After spraying the mist, with open hands, she sweeps the body's aura to smooth the energy.

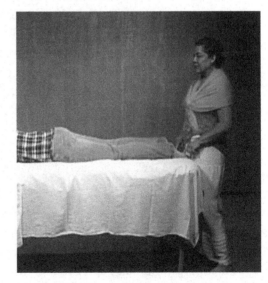

**Figure 20.1** Patricia is opening the power portal located on the feet as part of the Tonalli Cleansing.

3. **Opening the Power Portal:** Patricia moves to the feet area where the power portal is located, near the pads of the feet and near the toes. She massages this area by making small circles with her fingers clockwise and then counter clockwise five times.

   The portal area is tapped with her fingers three times. While pressing with her index finger on the portal area, Patricia asks the patient to take three deep breaths. The power portal is tapped a few more times in order to open it.

4. **Moving the Energy on the Back of the Body:** Patricia places her hand on the ankles, gently rocking them in order to prepare the body for the energy to move. She places her thumb and index finger (called the "power finger") just below the calve area, and begins rocking the leg in order to stimulate the energy. She reminds the patient to breath, models the breathing technique, and continues her rocking massage on the right side of the body, which is considered the masculine energetic side, while the left side is the feminine, an approach based on the Chinese *yin yang* and Mesoamerican *ometeotl* concept of duality. She continues moving up the calf making sure not to go into the groove of the knee. Using two fingers, she taps the center meridian of the calf three times and moves to the hip area. The thumb and power index finger are placed on each side of the hip and massaged in order to loosen the energy. Patricia tells us that this energetic area is connected to material things like finances and that it helps connect with the energy of *Madre Tierra,* Mother Earth. She places her hands on both sides of the hip, the iliac crest area, and begins gently rocking the body and moving to the back and shoulders. By this time, she begins to feel the energy moving.

5. **Moving the Energy on the Head and Front of the Body:** The patient is asked to turn and lay face-up. Patricia returns to the patient's feet and once more massages the power portal area, as describe on the above step three. This time, both Patricia and the patient can feel the energy moving. She moves in front of the patient, sits on a chair, and places her hands under the patient's occipital back and lower part of the cranium. The neck is slightly lifted and gently massaged to release tension and relax the head. She then places both middle fingers on the patient's third eye located in the middle of her forehead that provides perception beyond site and focuses on the patient's energy entering the mind's eye or third eye. In order to transmit Patricia's energy into the third eye, she places the tip of her tongue on the roof of her mouth and takes three deep breaths, feeling the energy pulsating into the patient's third eye. Patricia moves her hands down to the temples and performs small circular massage movements in order to activate the energy that has already traveled to the head. She moves to the ear and slightly bends it with her power index finger until she sees the crease, which is energy line that is the direction to the portal point on top of the head. In this area, Patricia makes small circular movements clockwise and asks the patient to think and focus on a white light entering her body, the energy entering her body. She then returns to the occipital back of the head where she feels more energy moving. By this time, Patricia and the patient can feel a looser and relaxed body with the tonalli energy moving freely.

**Conclusion:** Even though I have known my friend and colleague Patricia for several years, I had never observed and listened to her detailed process of a tonalli cleansing and the opening of the power portal that travels through the energetic meridian in a patient. I visited Patricia's My Madre Tierra clinic website and read a number of testimonials from patients who were very satisfied with her energy treatments. She is one of those unique healers, like the late Elena Avila, who realize their gifts as youngsters and continue developing their talents. I am glad that the state of Arizona has the services of Patricia Federico-Ruiz.

# CHAPTER 21
# Traditional Healing for Infants and the Aging Community

## 21.1 INTRODUCTION TO TRADITIONAL HEALING FOR INFANTS AND THE AGING COMMUNITY

Traditional healers Rita and Tonita have contributed to a number of chapters in this book. In the following sections, they will be dealing with two stages of life when our health needs may not be completely met. In the early stages of an infant's life, they communicate mostly with crying and shouting. The elderly may have limited income for health care, and illnesses like Dementia and Alzheimer's make it a challenge to serve their needs. Rita offers traditional ways of meeting the needs of both groups.

Dr. Thomas Armstrong, in **The Human Odyssey: Twelve Stages of the Human Life Cycle,** (2008) claims that some believe infancy is the most important stage of the human cycle since their experiences will determine the rest of their life. Others think that late adulthood is more important because of all the wisdom acquired; however, in terms of health needs, both of these stages of life are crucial, especially during birth and through early childhood of about six years of age. During this time, infants and young children are dependent on their parents for all of their health care. At the mature adult stage of about 50–80 years, and beyond, the aging process affects our physical and mental abilities as well as many of our organs.

My dad used to say, "Cheo, we are like machines and cars. As we get older, we breakdown and need periodic tuneups, and at times, even an overhaul and a new engine." As I age, these words seem very true to me, but there are things that Rita recommends for these two stages that will improve our lives as infants and elders.

## 21.2 TRADITIONAL HEALING FOR INFANTS

Rita enjoys a family of four grown children and thirteen grandkids, which has offered her much experience in providing for the health needs of infants. Growing up in a small rural traditional family, she learned from her mother and ancestors the skills for keeping infants healthy. She begins her presentation on traditional healing for infants by emphasizing the correct way of carrying and protecting an infant. Rita is concerned about not injuring the baby or the mother, especially the back

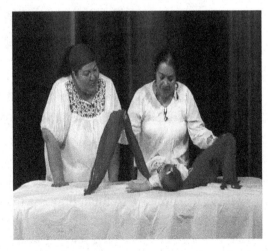

**Figure 21.1** Rita places a baby in a shawl as part of a rocking and soothing motion to relax the infant.

and cervical area, which includes bones, nerves, tendons, and ligaments that impact the neck area. One way to avoid injuring both mom and baby is to use a shawl in order to carry the baby, as is done by most of the women in her community.

The baby can also be placed on the shawl with the mom holding both ends while gently rocking the infant, as demonstrated in a previous chapter on the use of manteadas, or shawl alignments. Rita reminds us to avoid tossing the baby in the air so that it appears that the infant is laughing, when in reality the baby is scared and frightened.

The following are suggestions Rita makes in treating infants with traditional healing techniques:

1. **Pain:** Rita recommends that we hold an infant in a proper way to protect the baby from back pain. If we suspect a baby has back pain from constant crying, she recommends massaging a small amount of ointment prepared with medicinal herbs on the back and joints in order to alleviate the discomfort and relax the baby. After this is done, she suggests to wrap or swaddle the infant while gently tapping and continuing to massage the delicate body.

2. **Nursing:** Rita suggests that one should check on the baby's clicking of the tongue when the mom is nursing, quickly pulling the nipple out, since this is the cause of the infant taking in air that contributes to stomach inflammation and discomfort. The air can be eliminated by burping the baby.

3. **Teething:** Teething usually occurs at six months, but can happen as early as three. During this painful time, the gums are swollen, followed by fever or diarrhea, and the baby is cranky with lots of drooling. To ease the pain and inflammation, Rita recommends that the baby chew on a scallion onion.

4. **Respiratory Problems:** Rita recommends that the baby inhale the steam from a Eucalyptus tea for congestive and respiratory problems, and drink a small amount of diluted Borage tea if there is fever. If these problems are causing what may appear to be painful swallowing, she recommends a light massage starting at the chin, and moving toward the throat.

5. **Empacho:** Part 1 of this book discusses intestinal blockage called empacho. This constipation can be a result of digestive problems caused by the baby eating items such as paper or plastic. Rita suggests a gentle massage with clockwise circular motions on the stomach, followed by a teaspoon of olive oil. The baby's skin around the stomach is rolled and pulled in order to loosen the blockage. The baby is then turned, the back is lightly massaged, and the gentle pulling and rolling of the skin is continued.

6. **Other Traditional Ailments:** Rita names other traditional ailments but does not discuss them such as *caida de mollera*, known as a fallen or depressed fontanelle, which is the soft spot on the top of the baby's head. This illness can cause irritability, diarrhea, and vomiting. The second ailment is susto or espanto, related to fright, which could be caused by a number of things such as a fall, loud noise, or the bark of a dog. The symptoms could be irritability and uncontrollable crying.

**Conclusion:** Rita offers several traditional ways of healing infants that she learned in her village and from her ancestors. I am sure that she practiced these methods in raising her large family and grandchildren. As I traveled in Mexico to several communities, I observe healthy children wrapped in a shawl, or rebozo, and am impressed how this garment is so useful in the daily lives of women. I notice the love and caresses given to infants and babies. As these babies grow up, they seem to be more respectful of family values and they enjoy closer family ties. Could it be because they have fewer distractions such as TV, cell phones, computers, and electronics?

## 21.3 TRADITIONAL HEALING FOR THE AGING COMMUNITY

As we grow older, Rita realizes that our body is changing and suggests traditional means of staying healthy. In her clinic, she serves many elderly clients from age 50 and upwards and gets questions related to insomnia, stress, joint and muscle aches, constipation, and kidney/bladder issues. She receives complaints such as, "Once

I go to sleep, I can sleep perfectly well, but after an hour or two, I can't sleep anymore." Rita's response is to be conscience of what they eat in the evening that could interfere with their sleeping pattern. Rita addresses the following areas of concern with the aging community:

1. **Diet:** She correlates sleeping habits of the elderly to diet and promotes light evening meals such as oatmeal, with almonds or walnuts. Chewing food slowly and savoring each bite, avoiding sugars and caffeine drinks such as coffee, sodas, tea and substituting them with herbal teas like chamomile, ginger, *jamaica* (hibiscus flower) or mint, sweetening them with honey or stevia. Before an evening meal, she suggests a papaya and chia seed smoothie, which is rich in vitamins, minerals, fiber, and is both good for the digestive system and an excellent antioxidant.

2. **Skeletal System:** As the body ages, the bones in the skeletal system lose density and become more fragile and brittle. To take care of the bones and strengthen the collagen and calcium, Rita suggests a smoothie of amaranth seeds with walnuts or almonds and a half banana, which provides lots of minerals, vitamins, calcium, potassium in order to strengthen the immune system. Drinking horsetail tea or *cola de caballo*, contains silicone, which will strengthen the bones.

3. **Skin:** Rita is aware that the aging skin is thinner with a reduction in skin strength and elasticity and may show pigmented or age spots. In treating pain related to the back, shoulders, sciatica, or the lumbar region, she uses light treatments with fire cupping, as described in an earlier chapter, with the cup held for a few seconds in order to protect the delicate skin. Energetically hot plant oils are gently rubbed on the patient's skin for relaxation and to relieve the pain.

4. **Muscular System:** In order to improve muscular flexibility and allow the allow the heart to pump harder, since it slows down with age, Rita recommends physical activities in daily life such as walking and swimming, in order to keep their joints, muscles, and articulation moving. For frequent back pain around the spinal column, she uses a stronger herbal *malabar* oil, which has an analgesic effect.

5. **Knees:** Because of loss of cartilage or past injuries, she meets many elderly people with knee pain. Rita recommends a more relaxed exercise and a gentle massage with hot plant oil, in this case. She suggests appropriate and comfortable shoes to ease knee pain and avoid any falls and injuries.

6. **Dry Eyes:** The aging process, medications, and diseases can cause a slower tear flow and dry eyes. Rita recommends a warm compress of *manzanilla* (chamomile) tea placed on the eyes to relieve inflammation and provide moisture.

**Conclusion:** The normal aging process impacts our total body system such as the digestive, circulatory, and respiratory systems. Rita recommends several basic therapies to improve the changes that occur during these years such as better sleep, appropriate diet, relaxation exercises, physical activity, massage therapy, and medicinal herbs. With proper and adequate prevention and treatments, these body changes can be reversed for a better quality of life.

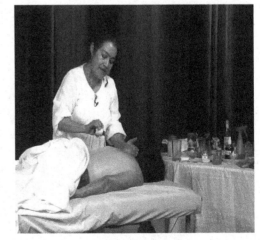

**Figure 21.2** Rita uses a hot plant oil to gently place on the patient's skin for relaxation and pain.

# CHAPTER 22

# Healing Grief through Day of the Dead (Dia de los Muertos)

I met Dr. Anselmo Torres Arismendi almost 20 years ago while he was a graduate student at the University of New Mexico. Before coming to New Mexico he was an administrator in the College of Nursing at the state university of Cuernavaca. After receiving his degree, he enrolled in a second graduate program in Paris, France, through the United Nations Educational, Scientific, and Cultural Organization (UNESCO) program. He returned to New Mexico and completed his PhD and then taught university classes while helping me with a number of initiatives with Mexican colleges and universities. He currently teaches in higher education in Mexico and continues being part of the curanderismo classes by teaching the healing of grief through the Day of the Dead/*Dia de los Muertos* celebration.

I have joined him in several Day of the Dead celebrations in Mexican communities such as San Andres Mixquic outside of Mexico City and in Morelia, Michoacan. In San Andres Mixquic, we joined hundreds of Mexican visitors at the Alumbrada in the cemetery next to the community church, and enjoyed many beautiful altars/*ofrendas*, thousands of candles, and aromas from burning copal incense. This area has been designated as a *Barrio Magico* or Magical Neighborhood.

After midnight, we spend a few hours visiting family members at another cemetery for an all-night vigil where I learned to respect the devotion and meaning of this celebration. I had a similar experience in Morelia, Michoacan, where we visited a number of cemeteries including homes where loved ones gathered to pray, eat, dance, and remember those who had died. At both places I could feel the spirits during the festivities, which included the wonderful aroma of yellow marigold flowers called *cempasuchitl*, and rows of candles for the purpose of attracting and illuminating a path for the spirits on their arrival.

In his presentation to the students in the curanderismo class, Anselmo reminds us that the Day of the Dead festival is celebrated on October 31st through November 2nd throughout Mexico, but mostly in Central and the Southern regions, and even in the United States in communities with large numbers of Latinos, especially from Mexico. Generally, November 1st honors infants and children who have passed and the day is called *Dia de los Inocentes* or *Angelitos*/Day of the Innocent or Little Angels, while November 2nd recognizes deceased adults and is called *Dia de los Santos*/All Saints Day. November 2nd is *Dia de*

**Figure 22.1** Dr. Anselmo Torres, from Mexico City, provides insight on the meanings and significances of one of Mexico's most important celebrations, the Day of the Dead.

*los Difuntos*/Day of the Dead or All Souls Day, when families go to the cemeteries to clean and decorate the graves and tombs. For more than 20 years, Albuquerque, New Mexico has celebrated this holiday on November 2nd in the South Valley with a parade, altars, music, and art.

In his presentations on the Day of the Dead, Anselmo shares the following information:

1. **Brief History:** In the Mesoamerican native culture, there were two kinds of worlds: the horizontal one, where the earth is located, and the vertical one which has thirteen skies or heavens, and nine netherworlds or "hells." The Aztecs believed they were immortals and that death was actually another stage of life. The belief was that during a certain time in the year, their spirits would return to earth and join their families for a few hours before returning to one of their worlds.

2. **Meaning of Day of the Dead/Dia de los Muertos:** Anselmo tells us, "What do we do when we have visitors or guests in our homes? We tidy up and make sure they are welcomed with food and drinks and we may dance with them." According to the traditions, we celebrate because the gods have allowed the spirits of our love ones from one of the thirteen heavens and nine underworld/netherworlds to return to earth for a visit. The relatives and friends can prepare to receive the spirit of their love ones by cleaning the tombs at the cemetery, setting up altars with bright yellow marigold flowers and candles, to light their journey to earth, and by preparing food with sugar skulls, as well desserts and drinks that they enjoyed on earth. As a reminder, love ones can have photos and memorabilia related to the deceased.

3. **Grieving:** This celebration allows the relatives to celebrate in a spiritual way and to help work on the stages of grief. We can live with them for three days (October 31st–November 2nd) therefore working out any blocked emotions. There is also a collective and community celebration to welcome back the spirits.

4. **The Altar:** Anselmo's PowerPoint presentation describes the altars of earlier years that included a pyramid shape and three levels covered with colored paper. The first level had photos of the loved ones, the second level had food, flowers, candles, and copal, and the third one was on the ground level with a foliage path of yellow marigold flowers and lit candles.

When the Spaniards arrived, the new Catholic religion introduced saints, crucifixes, and new fruits. The three levels represented the father, son, and holy spirit and the marigold or *cempasuchitl* flower was used for death and strength of sunlight. Fruits with small flags on top symbolized the freedom that death brings, favorite foods were believed to be carried to the other life, candles lit the path for the spirit, and copal incense scared away any evil spirit.

**Figure 22.2** The altar, with its *ofrendas*, has changed throughout the years and honors the memories of loved ones.

**Conclusion:** We all experience grief in our lives and it is never completely over. The traditional Day of the Dead celebration allows us to remember our loved ones once a year and to celebrate their contributions that they made when they were on earth. Other cultures such as the Africans, Chinese, and Japanese have similar beliefs about tending to the graves of loved ones and the belief that their spirits visit them. During the class session on the Day of the Dead, the students are offered the option of creating an altar and most of them participate. Here are some of their comments, "My husband passed away seven years ago and was a cigar smoker, to my dismay. Now I brought a cigar to the altar to remind me of how much I miss him." Another student says, "This is the photo of my dog, my best friend, who helped me recover from a major illness."

# CONCLUSION

**B**ecause of the recent interest of traditional medicine as well as other health modalities such as complementary, alternative, or integrative medicine, I decided to teach a course at the University of New Mexico on "Traditional Medicine without Borders: Curanderismo in the Southwest and Mexico" many years ago. This course, plus an online class on the same topic, has grown in popularity and enrolled student and presenters from throughout the country and other parts of the world. This publication serves as a supplement to the class, and will provide information to readers interested in learning more about the medicine of our ancestors and the influences from other cultures that have enriched curanderismo.

I hope that you have enjoyed Part 1 with its emphasis on **Curanderismo of the Southwest and Mexico**, beginning with a chapter on my mentor and teacher, Chenchito, who is one of the last survivors of the original group of followers of the Fidencista healing movement based on the teachings and traditional spiritual healings of the famous Niño Fidencio who lived in the early 1900s. You have also learned about popular medicinal plants of the Southwest, those for the digestive and nervous system, and how to prepare some of these plants in alcohol-based tinctures and water-based micro-dosages.

You have learned a number of spiritual or energetic cleansings, and the tools used for them such as certain plants and *copal* incense. Ancient and revived healing methods have been explained, such as cures for intestinal blockage (empacho), shawl alignment (manteadas), fire cupping (ventosas) and Mesoamerican sweat lodges (temazcals). The first part ends with the knowledge of healing with the earth (Geotherapy), and healing with laughter, sound, and music.

You have learned in Part 2 of this book the global perspectives of traditional medicine from countries such as Uganda, Gabon, Cuba, Puerto Rico, Peru, and Mexico. Healers from Uganda and Gabon, Africa, have shared their traditional medicine with us through medicinal plants and music. We have read the healing influences and contributions from the African diaspora in a chapter called "Contributions of Afro-Latino Healing," which described the African healing belief system introduced to Cuba and Puerto Rico as well as healing music and dance. From the South American country of Peru, a shaman/*curandero* has shared with us the sacred use of tobacco in healing therapies.

We have learned from two indigenous groups, the use of Native American feather healing for spiritual cleansings and Mayan acupuncture and abdominal massage techniques. Traditional chiropractors without formal training have shared with us the skills of a bonesetter, a body adjustment, and a spinal alignment. We have learned the simple method of healing with water called hydrotherapy and ways of moving the body's energy, called tonalli.

Two groups in our society that require special attention are infants and the elderly and we discovered how to provide traditional health services in a section, entitled, "Traditional Healing for Infants and the Aging Community." Finally, we learned how to grieve and remember the death of a loved one in the chapter, "Healing Grief through Day of the Dead."

I hope that this book has given you information and appreciation of simple but effective ways that our ancestors utilized to address their health needs. We realize that allopathic modern medicine has excellent cures and advances and we should see a health provider for our needs. However, there are traditional methods that could be beneficial, if done correctly and do not harm you, especially in healing our soul and spirit.

# REFERENCES

**FILM:**

Echevarria, Nicolas. (1980). *El Niño Fidencio: El Taumaturgo de Espinazo* (Documentary Film). Mexico: Centro de Producción de Cortometraje.

**BOOKS, JOURNALS, PERIODICALS:**

Armstrong, T. (2008). *The Human Odyssey: Navigating the Twelve Stages of Life.* New York City: Sterling Publishing.

Berk, L. S., Tan, S. A., Fry, W. F., Napier, B. J., Lee, J. W., Hubbard, R.W., & Eby, W. C. (1989). Neuroendocrine and Stress Hormone Changes during Mirthful Laughter. *The American Journal of the Medical Sciences, 298*(6), 390–396.

Cousins, N. (2005). *Anatomy of an Illness as Perceived by the Patient: Reflections on Healing and Regeneration.* New York City: W.W. Norton and Co.

Friedman, M. (2014, February 4). Does Music Have Healing Powers? *Psychology Today.* Retrieved From: https://www.psychologytoday.com/.

Gates, W. (2012). *An Aztec Herbal: The Classic Codex of 1552.* North Chelmsford: Courier Corporation.

Saber, A. (2010). Ancient Egyptian Surgical Heritage. *Journal of Investigative Surgery, 23*(6), 327–334.

Schwartz, G. (2009). What Energy Healing Can Do For You. *Bottom Line: Health.* 11–12.

Struthers, R., & Hodge, F. S. (2004). Sacred tobacco use in Ojibwe communities. *Journal of Holistic Nursing, 22*(3), 209–225.

Torres, E. (2005). *Curandero: A Life in Mexican Folk Healing.* Albuquerque: University of New Mexico Press.

Torres, E. (2006). *Healing with Herbs and Rituals: A Mexican Tradition.* Albuquerque: University of New Mexico Press.

Trotter, R., & Chavira, J. A. (2011). *Curanderismo: Mexican-American Folk healing.* Athens: University of Georgia Press.

Vetter, R. & Tartsah, R. Jr. (2012). *Big Bow: The Spiritual Life and Teachings of a Kiowa Family.* East Port: World Journeys Publishing.

**IMAGES**

*Figure 1.* Curanderismo in the Southwest and Mexico [Video File]. 2015. Retrieved from the University of New Mexico, Extended Learning. Blackboard: learn.unm.edu.

*Figure 2.* Chenchito Interview [Video File]. 2015. Retrieved from the University of New Mexico, Extended Learning. Blackboard: learn.unm.edu.

*Figure 3.* El Nino Fidencio Documentary [Video File]. 2015. Retrieved from the University of New Mexico. Extended Learning. Blackboard: learn.unm.edu.

Echevarria, N., Sheridan, Guilermo. (1980). *Figure 4 Nino Fidencio: El taumaturgo de Espinazo.* [Screenshot of Documentary]. Mexico: Centro de Produccion de Cortometraje.

*Figure 5.* Chenchito Interview [Video File]. 2015. Retrieved from the University of New Mexico. Extended Learning. Blackboard: learn.unm.edu.

*Figure 6.* Plants of the Southwest [Video File]. 2015. Retrieved from the University of New Mexico. Extended Learning. Blackboard: learn.unm.edu.

*Figure 7.* Medicinal Plants for the Digestive System [Video File]. 2015. Retrieved from the University of New Mexico. Extended Learning. Blackboard: learn.unm.edu.

*Figure 8.* Medicinal Plants for the Nervous System [Video File]. 2015. Retrieved from the University of New Mexico. Extended Learning. Blackboard: learn.unm.edu.

*Figure 9.* Tinctures & Microdosis [Video File]. 2015. Retrieved from the University of New Mexico. Extended Learning. Blackboard: learn.unm.edu.

*Figure 10* Juice Therapy [Video File]. 2015. Retrieved from the University of New Mexico. Extended Learning. Blackboard: learn.unm.edu.

Nunez, D. M. (Photographer of Image). (February 2017). *Figure 11. Amulets for Protection* [Photo File]. University of New Mexico.

*Figure 12.* Spiritual Healing [Video File]. 2015. Retrieved from the University of New Mexico. Extended Learning. Blackboard: learn.unm.edu.

*Figure 13.* Healing Fright and Shock [Video File]. 2015. Retrieved from the University of New Mexico. Extended Learning. Blackboard: learn.unm.edu.

*Figure 14.* Spiritual Cleansings [Video File]. 2015. Retrieved from the University of New Mexico. Extended Learning. Blackboard: learn.unm.edu.

*Figure 15.* Burning Incense for Harmonizing [Video File]. 2016. Retrieved from the University of New Mexico. Extended Learning. Blackboard: learn.unm.edu.

*Figure 16.* Intestinal Blockage [Video File]. 2015. Retrieved from the University of New Mexico. Extended Learning. Blackboard: learn.unm.edu.

*Figure 17.* Shawl Alignment [Video File]. 2015. Retrieved from the University of New Mexico. Extended Learning. Blackboard: learn.unm.edu.

*Figure 18.* Fire Cupping [Video File]. 2015. Retrieved from the University of New Mexico. Extended Learning. Blackboard: learn.unm.edu.

*Figure 19.* Geotherapy [Video File]. 2015. Retrieved from the University of New Mexico. Extended Learning. Blackboard: learn.unm.edu.

*Figure 20.* Healing with Herbal Oils [Video File]. 2016. Retrieved from the University of New Mexico. Extended Learning. Blackboard: learn.unm.edu.

Gonzales, A. (Photographer for Image). October 2014. *Figure 21.* [Photo File]. Temazcal Tonantzin. Albuquerque, New Mexico.

*Figure 22.* Temazcal 3 of 3 [Video File]. 2015. Retrieved from the University of New Mexico. Extended Learning. Blackboard: learn.unm.edu.

*Figure 23.* Laugh Therapy [Video File]. 2015. Retrieved from the University of New Mexico. Extended Learning. Blackboard: learn.unm.edu.

*Figure 24.* Healing through Sound [Video File]. 2015. Retrieved from the University of New Mexico. Extended Learning. Blackboard: learn.unm.edu.

*Figure 25.* Healing through Music [Video File]. 2015. Retrieved from the University of New Mexico. Extended Learning. Blackboard: learn.unm.edu.

*Figure 26.* African Traditional Healing [Video File]. 2015. Retrieved from the University of New Mexico. Extended Learning. Blackboard: learn.unm.edu.

*Figure 27.* African Healing through Music [Video File]. 2015. Retrieved from the University of New Mexico. Extended Learning. Blackboard: learn.unm.edu.

*Figure 28.* Afro-Latino Healing through Music and Dance [Video File]. 2015. Retrieved from the University of New Mexico. Extended Learning. Blackboard: learn.unm.edu.

*Figure 29.* Afro-Cuban [Video File]. 2015. Retrieved from the University of New Mexico. Extended Learning. Blackboard: learn.unm.edu.

*Figure 30.* Afro-Puerto Rican [Video File]. 2015. Retrieved from the University of New Mexico. Extended Learning. Blackboard: learn.unm.edu.

*Figure 31.* Sacred Tobacco of Peru [Video File]. 2015. Retrieved from the University of New Mexico. Extended Learning. Blackboard: learn.unm.edu.

*Figure 32.* Herbal Smoke for Healing [Video File]. 2015. Retrieved from the University of New Mexico. Extended Learning. Blackboard: learn.unm.edu.

*Figure 33.* Creating a Sacred Space for Healing [Video File]. 2015. Retrieved from the University of New Mexico. Extended Learning. Blackboard: learn.unm.edu.

*Figure 34.* Creating a Sacred Space for Healing [Video File]. 2015. Retrieved from the University of New Mexico. Extended Learning. Blackboard: learn.unm.edu.

*Figure 35.* Feather Healing [Video File]. 2015. Retrieved from the University of New Mexico. Extended Learning. Blackboard: learn.unm.edu.

*Figure 36.* Huesero [Video File]. 2015. Retrieved from the University of New Mexico. Extended Learning. Blackboard: learn.unm.edu.

*Figure 37.* Mayan Acupuncture [Video File]. 2015. Retrieved from the University of New Mexico. Extended Learning. Blackboard: learn.unm.edu.

*Figure 38.* Mayan Abdominal Massage [Video File]. 2015. Retrieved from the University of New Mexico. Extended Learning. Blackboard: learn.unm.edu.

*Figure 39.* Body Adjustment [Video File]. 2015. Retrieved from the University of New Mexico. Extended Learning. Blackboard: learn.unm.edu.

*Figure 40.* Spinal Alignment [Video File]. 2015. Retrieved from the University of New Mexico. Extended Learning. Blackboard: learn.unm.edu.

*Figure 41.* Healing with Water [Video File]. 2015. Retrieved from the University of New Mexico. Extended Learning. Blackboard: learn.unm.edu.

*Figure 42.* Healing with Water [Video File]. 2015. Retrieved from the University of New Mexico. Extended Learning. Blackboard: learn.unm.edu.

*Figure 43.* Cleansing Tonalli [Video File]. 2015. Retrieved from the University of New Mexico. Extended Learning. Blackboard: learn.unm.edu.

*Figure 44.* Traditional Remedies for Infants and Children [Video File]. 2015. Retrieved from the University of New Mexico. Extended Learning. Blackboard: learn.unm.edu.

*Figure 45.* Traditional Healing for the Aging Community [Video File]. 2015. Retrieved from the University of New Mexico. Extended Learning. Blackboard: learn.unm.edu.

*Figure 46.* Healing Grief through Day of the Dead [Video File]. 2015. Retrieved from the University of New Mexico. Extended Learning. Blackboard: learn.unm.edu.

*Figure 47.* Healing Grief through Day of the Dead [Video File]. 2015. Retrieved from the University of New Mexico. Extended Learning. Blackboard: learn.unm.edu.

# INDEX